What Makes Our Relationships Meaningful, Satisfying, or Fulfilling?

Also by Thomas G. Kirkpatrick

Small Groups in the Church: A Handbook for Creating Community

Communication in the Church: A Handbook for Healthier Relationships

Better Ways to Better Relationships in the Church: Guidelines for Practicing Humility, Experiencing Empathy, Feeling Compassion, Showing Kindness, Expressing Appreciation, and Doing Justice

Signs of Hope and Health in Mainline Churches: Guidelines for Creating Hopeful and Healthy Congregations

What Makes Our Relationships Meaningful, Satisfying, or Fulfilling?

Answers from Social Scientists and the Wisdom of Ordinary People

THOMAS G. KIRKPATRICK

WIPF & STOCK · Eugene, Oregon

WHAT MAKES OUR RELATIONSHIPS MEANINGFUL, SATISFYING, OR FULFILLING?
Answers from Social Scientists and the Wisdom of Ordinary People

Copyright © 2025 Thomas G. Kirkpatrick. All rights reserved. Except for brief quotations in critical publications or reviews, no part of this book may be reproduced in any manner without prior written permission from the publisher. Write: Permissions, Wipf and Stock Publishers, 199 W. 8th Ave., Suite 3, Eugene, OR 97401.

Wipf & Stock
An Imprint of Wipf and Stock Publishers
199 W. 8th Ave., Suite 3
Eugene, OR 97401

www.wipfandstock.com

PAPERBACK ISBN: 979-8-3852-6553-4
HARDCOVER ISBN: 979-8-3852-6554-1
EBOOK ISBN: 979-8-3852-6555-8

VERSION NUMBER 12/15/25

Contents

Acknowledgments | vii
Introduction | ix

1. What Makes Our Relationships Meaningful, Fulfilling, and Satisfying? | 1
2. What Makes Our Relationships Meaningful, Satisfying, or Fulfilling? | 20
3. What Makes Our Relationships Meaningful, Satisfying, or Fulfilling? | 35
4. Making Relationships Meaningful, Satisfying, or Fulfilling | 58

About the Author | 89
Appendix 1: Relationship Science: An Overview | 91
Appendix 2: Research Project Summary: 1975 | 93
Appendix 3: Interpersonal Relationship Satisfaction Inventory (IRSI) | 97
Appendix 4: Interpersonal Relationship Satisfaction Inventory (IRSI Short Form) | 102
Appendix 5: Four C's Signs of Relational Health | 105
Appendix 6: Meaningful, Satisfying, or Fulfilling Relationships Themes (Percent and Number of Respondents) | 107

Appendix 7: Theme-Related Word Usage (Percent and Number of Respondent Word Usage) | 111
Appendix 8: Meaningful, Satisfying, or Fulfilling Relationships Themes Components | 113
Appendix 9: MSF Relationships Inventory (Ten Themes) | 116
Appendix 10: Meaningful, Satisfying, and Fulfilling Word Usage (Percent and Number of Respondent Word Usage) | 118
Appendix 11: Questionnaire Questions | 120
Appendix 12: Questionnaires Results | 125
Appendix 13: Brief Reflections and Mini-Case Studies | 137
Appendix 14: Relationship Satisfaction Inventory (RSI) | 148
Bibliography | 151

Acknowledgments

I AM DEEPLY GRATEFUL to the following people:
Members of two support groups, one personal and one professional, for their support and enthusiasm for this research and writing project.

Members of my family, especially my wife, Carol, and my children and their partners, Matt, Michele, Chris and Samantha, and Juliann and Lawrence. Their ongoing interest in and wholehearted appreciation for my calling as a researcher and writer are deeply appreciated gifts!

Matthew Wimer and his Wipf and Stock editorial and publication teams, for their rare and unwavering commitment to publish books based on merit.

I am especially grateful to family members, friends, and colleagues for their permission to use the following:

Quotations: Joan Ackerman, John Asher, Kathryn Castle, Susan Covey, Cheryl Drinkwine, Jim Drinkwine, Linda Flatley, Al Gephart, Tom Hill, Kathy Johnstone, Liz Kearny, Chris Kirkpatrick, Henry Kirkpatrick, LeAnn Kirkpatrick, Kurt Kirkpatrick, Mary Ann Kirkpatrick, Michele Kirkpatrick, Sage Kirkpatrick, Steve Kirkpatrick, John Lofstedt, Ron Marshall, Janelle McCarty, Angela Miksovsky, Jack Pauw, Natasha Pauw, Jenni Porter, Connie Riggle, Riley Roberts, Jackson Stewart, Juliann Stewart, Les Stewart, Royce Stewart, James Tweedie, Pat Williams, and Josh Young.

Acknowledgments

Vignettes: Carol Anway, Alyssa Bennett, Joyce Carr, Kathryn Castle, Abbey Cox, Karen Dalton, Tim Devine, Linda Flatley, Al Gephart, Suzy Graham, Becky Grossmann, Katie Haney, Scott Hubbard, Gordon Jackson, Charlie Kirkpatrick, Heather Kirkpatrick, Joel Kirkpatrick, Seth Kirkpatrick, Travis Kirkpatrick, Jan Leng, Ernie Mathes, Paul McCann, Kari McFarland, Mark McHugh, Carol Ortiz, Irvin Porter, Tyler Roberts, and Rachel Young.

Reflections: John Asher, Susan Covey, Cheryl Drinkwine, Dexter Kearny, Rhonda Kirkpatrick, Lynn Longfield, Merrie McIvor, Barb Rolfe, Juliann Stewart, and Pat Willians.

Case Studies: Alice Davis, Karen Jacobson, Kathy Johnstone, Chris Kirkpatrick, Kyle Kirkpatrick, Larry Kirkpatrick, Margie Kirkpatrick, Mary Ann Kirkpatrick, Ann Lofstedt, Lawrence Stewart, and James Tweedie.

Other family members, friends, and colleagues who contributed answers to the research question include: Lara Allison, David Ammons, Delwin Andrews, MacKenna Bean, Neil Bolkcom, Suzanne Brown, Carol Dunford, Joyce Martin Emery, Chloe Hackett, Jessie Cornwell, Carole Curtis, Dorothy Ferguson, Duncan Ferguson, Linda Gaines, Kyian Hedrick, Randy Henderson, Sandy Hill, Harlan Hilman, Margaret Johnson, Doug Karman, James Kim, Carol Kirkpatrick, Ed Kirkpatrick, Ryan Kirkpatrick, Samantha Kirkpatrick, Scott Kramer, Diane Lee, Karen Lenstra, Myra Marshall, Sheri Martin, Mike McCarty, Joyce North, Tom Paine, Merry Pantaleo, Jane Pauw, Ben Pierce, Barb Petit, Craig Riggle, Savanna Roberts, Sophey Roberts, Trevor Roney, Colleen Russell, James Schiller, Sid Sidell, Halley Starr, John Steppert, Kathryn Stewart, Cheri Stutz, Pat Todhunter, Ann Wiltse, Dwight Wipple, Jerry Wiggins-Ackerson, Susan Wiggins-Ackerson, and John Worcester.

It is to all these family members, friends, and colleagues that I dedicate this book.

Introduction

THIS BOOK FEATURES A unique research project: it spans fifty years. It seeks to replicate in 2025 findings from research in 1975 that asks this question: What makes our relationships meaningful, satisfying, or fulfilling?

The original project began with my graduate studies in the Department of Communication at the University of Washington in the mid-1970s. I remember walking into a near-vacant Parrington Hall in the summer of 1974 and calling out, "Is anybody here?" A quiet voice from a backroom office called out, "Yes, come on in!" Then department chair Dr. Thomas Nilsen welcomed my query about the department's offerings. In one of those "being-at-the-right-place-at-the-right-time" moments in life, I learned that the Department of Communication was adding a new emphasis area to its programs in rhetoric and public address, speech and hearing science, and the oral interpretation of literature: interpersonal and small group communication. This new discipline was exactly what I wanted to study. I learned a great deal about the practice of interpersonal and small group communication from my recently completed work in campus ministry. And I was looking to add the academic side to what I'd learned in my practice of ministry. For example, I wanted to learn what makes our relationships meaningful, satisfying, or fulfilling.

In fact, I was able to conduct a research project focused on this question. The results of this research were presented in a

Introduction

peer-reviewed paper at the Western Speech Communication Association Convention in Phoenix, Arizona, November 20–23, 1977, titled "Conceptualizing and Measuring Relationship Satisfaction." The introduction to this paper serves as a starting point for my research fifty years ago in 1975, and sets the stage for our research now fifty years later in 2025:

> The attainment of satisfying relationships with other people is generally regarded as a highly valued human experience. Even a moment's reflection suggests that we are dependent upon others for the satisfaction of such strong desires as love, approval, and esteem. Furthermore, satisfying human relationships are sought by acquaintances, friends, and intimates; in one-to-one, group, and organizational settings; and inside and outside the communication consultant's office. But given that the experience of relationship satisfaction is important, the student of interpersonal behavior must isolate the relevant variables if the frontiers of knowledge are to recede. The communication researcher must ask: "What makes interpersonal relationships satisfying?"[1]

My original research discovered that these four factors are what make our relationships meaningful, satisfying, or fulfilling: *communication openness, being oneself, interpersonal security and warmth, and personal support and growth.* I also developed a forty-item Interpersonal Relationships Satisfaction Inventory (IRSI) measurement instrument. And I would go on to use a twelve-item short version in my DMin dissertation research on conceptualizing and developing community in a congregation.

Now, fifty years later, I became curious about whether or not these same four factors are still predictors or determinants of meaningful, satisfying, or fulfilling relationships. So, I conducted a new research project using the same research question and a similar research design to see if I could replicate my findings from fifty years ago. My initial research involved three hundred subjects: 180

---

1. Kirkpatrick, "Conceptualizing and Measuring Relationship Satisfaction" (paper presented at Western Speech Communication Association Convention, Phoenix, Arizona, November 20–23, 1977), 1.

Introduction

from speech communication classes at the University of Washington and 120 from nearby Presbyterian (USA) congregations. Since I no longer have access to university students, I recruited 191 family members, friends, good friends, and colleagues in my new research. I asked for one or two (or more) brief responses to the research question. A typical response was "That's a great question," "It is thought-provoking," "Thank you for asking," "Here's my answer," and "I hope it is helpful." In other words, it became apparent that there is a wave of interest or felt need, perhaps even a "hot topic"—one in which participants saw themselves as stakeholders in the research.

Their answers were helpful, indeed! Many were wise, and some quite profound. And they replicate three of the original four factors: communication openness, being oneself, and personal support and growth. Interpersonal security and warmth was missing. However, ten themes emerge from participant responses, seven of which are new: communication, being oneself, and growth along with connection, mutuality, enjoyment, time, work, presence, and transcendence. A new Meaningful, Satisfying, or Fulfilling (MSF) Relationship Satisfaction Inventory was developed as a measurement instrument for these ten themes. Also, a Relationship Satisfaction Inventory was developed to measure the construct, relationship satisfaction.

After completing the new research project, several fresh questions surfaced and a follow-up research project designed. For example, how are respondents doing in their meaningful, satisfying, or fulfilling relationships with respect to the four factors and ten themes? In other words, to what extent can they be open in their communication, be themselves, experience interpersonal security and warmth, and experience personal support and growth? And to what extent do they connect with people; have mutual interests; enjoy being together; communicate well; spend time together; feel free to be themselves; learn and grow; work at their relationships; be present and available to one another; and feed their souls and spirits?

Introduction

Also, in asking these questions, how should the words "meaningful," "satisfying," and "fulfilling" be defined? And by whom—the respondents or myself? Respondents were asked to define *meaningful, satisfying,* or *fulfilling* (hereafter m/s/f) relationships, both in order to gain fresh insight about the meaning of each word and to learn what they mean to respondents as they respond to related research questions. In addition, each respondent was asked the extent to which their m/s/f relationships "have significance, value, or importance" (my definition for *meaningful* relationships), "bring enjoyment, pleasure, or contentment" (my definition for *satisfying* relationships), and "thrive or flourish" (my definition for *fulfilling* relationships).

Additional questions include: How many m/s/f relationships do respondents have? And among what types of personal relationships are most respondents' m/s/f relationships—family members, friends, good friends, colleagues, or a combination of these types of personal relationships? Also, how do respondents rate the overall health of their m/s/f relationships?

A central issue in this study is how best to define "meaningful," "satisfying," and "fulfilling" relationships. Whereas there are distinct dictionary-type meanings for each word as well as distinct understandings in the social science literature, participants in the follow-up study don't seem to make nuanced distinctions and even seem to use them interchangeably or jointly.

Most personal relationships for all respondents are among their family members and good friends. Their relationships as a whole are very meaningful, satisfying, or fulfilling, and the overall health of their relationships is relatively high. Also, respondents are quite able to be open in their communication, be themselves, experience interpersonal security and warmth, and experience personal support and growth in their personal relationships. Likewise, they are quite able to connect; have mutual interests; enjoy being together; communicate well; spend time together; feel free to be themselves; learn and grow; work at their relationships; be present and available; and feed their souls and spirits. And these positive results even extend to specific ways respondents experience each of the four factors and ten themes.

Introduction

OVERVIEW OF THIS BOOK

Chapter 1 answers the research question from the perspectives of social scientists. Nuanced understandings of *meaningful, fulfilling,* and *satisfying* relationships evolve.

Chapter 2 answers our question from the experience and wisdom of ordinary people. It summarizes the original research from 1975 and the attempt now, fifty years later, to replicate the original findings. Specifically, we'll learn if what makes our relationships meaningful, satisfying, or fulfilling now in 2025 is the same as it was fifty years ago.

Chapter 3 answers follow-up questions that arise from the previous researches. This follow-up research explores how participants are doing in their four relational qualities and their ten relational themes, seeks fresh insights about the meaning of m/s/f relationships, and learns the number, type, and health of respondents' m/s/f relationships. A new, eclectic theory of m/s/f personal relationships is also introduced.

And in chapter 4 we'll learn how to make our relationships meaningful, satisfying, or fulfilling. Practical ways of making them so are outlined for our four qualities and ten themes drawing on insights from social scientists and our three research projects. And the wisdom of ordinary people is featured with forty short quotations, thirty vignettes, ten brief reflections, and ten mini-case studies. This book closes with conclusions drawn from what we've learned in this chapter and the previous three chapters about how to make our relationships meaningful, satisfying, or fulfilling.

You will find practical application study guides at the end of each chapter. Further resources include chapter footnotes, appendices, and a bibliography at the back of the book.

My family members, friends, and colleagues got it right: we're asking a great and thought-provoking question, and their wisdom, along with that of our social scientists, is exceedingly helpful in expanding our understanding and practice of making relationships meaningful, satisfying, or fulfilling!

1

What Makes Our Relationships Meaningful, Fulfilling, and Satisfying?

This road [Positive Psychology] takes you through the countryside of pleasure and gratification, up into the high country of strength and virtue, and finally to the peaks of lasting fulfillment: meaning and purpose.

—MARTIN E. P. SELIGMAN

ANSWERS FROM SOCIAL SCIENTISTS

Meaningful Relationships

MICHAEL STEGER, FOUNDER AND director of the Center for Meaning and Purpose, and Pninit Russo-Netzer, head of the Compass Institute for the Study and Application of Meaning, suggest there

What Makes Our Relationships Meaningful, Satisfying, or Fulfilling? are three main types of meaning: significance, purpose, and coherence:[1]

- "Significance" means life is worth living, that one's life has inherent value, and that one matters in some way.
- "Purpose" means that there is something important we want to strive for, something that is worthy of the life we've been given.
- "Coherence" means that we can make sense of life, that we understand ourselves and the world around us, helping us see life as consistent and predictable most of the time.

Here's how psychology professor Daryl R. Van Tongeren and clinical social worker Sara A. Showalter Van Tongeren describe these three facets of meaning in their book *The Courage to Suffer: A New Clinical Framework for Life's Greatest Crises*: "Coherence *translates* events in ways that make sense; significance helps people *transcend* themselves and connect with others; and purpose *transforms* experience ... into something greater."[2]

Psychologist Jill Suttie identifies four keys to a meaningful life, based on a book by journalist Emily Esfahani Smith, *The Power of Meaning: Crafting a Life that Matters*. While significance is omitted, purpose and storytelling (coherence) are included along with two additional "pillars" of meaning, belonging and transcendence:[3]

- "Belonging" means we are understood, recognized, and affirmed by friends, family members, partners, colleagues, and even strangers—for many people, relationships are the most meaningful part of their lives.
- "Transcendence" means experiences that fill us with awe or wonder—they make us feel that we rise above the everyday world to experience a higher reality.

---

1. See Steger and Russo-Netzer, "To Have Your Best Life."

2. See Van Tongeren and Van Tongeren, *Courage to Suffer*, 9. Emphasis original.

3. See Suttie, "Four Keys to a Meaningful Life."

What Makes Our Relationships Meaningful, Fulfilling, and Satisfying?

The relationship between a meaningful life and a happy life is also an important one when considering what makes life worth living. For example, is a meaningful life different from a happy life? Often they go hand in hand, but not always. In a *Greater Good Magazine* article, "Is a Happy Life Different from a Meaningful One?," Jill Suttie and *Greater Good* Editor in Chief Jason Marsh point to research by psychologist Roy Baumeister and his colleagues who discovered that while happiness is connected to health, wealth, and ease in life, meaning in life is not. They also identified five major differences between a happy life and a meaningful one:[4]

- While happy people satisfy their wants and needs, these pursuits are irrelevant to a meaningful life.
- Happiness is fleeting while meaningfulness seems long-lasting.
- Meaningfulness comes from what one gives to others while happiness comes from what others give oneself.
- Engaging in challenging or difficult situations beyond oneself or one's pleasures promotes meaningfulness but not happiness.
- Self-expression is important to meaning but not happiness.

New research finds that kind and helpful behaviors can make our lives feel more meaningful. They create a sense of meaning we all seek. Giving helps us feel connected to others. For example, making others feel appreciated helps build our relationships with them and thereby makes our lives more meaningful. Research by Van Tongeren and colleagues finds such prosocial behavior and meaning in life were linked, in part, by the quality of people's relationships—by their relationship satisfaction.[5] Other research by Van Tongeren and psychology professor Jeni Burnette also finds that happiness mindsets are associated with greater wellbeing

---

4. See Suttie and Marsh, "Is a Happy Life."
5. See Van Tongeren et al. "Prosociality Enhances Meaning in Life," 225–36.

and greater relationship satisfaction.[6] We will consider these links between meaning in life, happiness, wellbeing, and relationship satisfaction later in this chapter.

We will also consider the relationship between a fulfilling life and happiness later in this chapter.

Jill Suttie also points to a relationship between meaning in life and having a sense of purpose. In another *Greater Good Magazine* article, "Seven Ways to Find Your Purpose in Life," she suggests that people who blend their talents, passion, and care for the world find meaning in their lives. Moreover, having purpose in life is good for our wellbeing. For example, she points out, "Having a purpose in life is associated with all kinds of benefits. Research suggests that purpose is tied to having better health, longevity, and even economic success. It feels good to have a sense of purpose, knowing that you are using your skills to help others in a way that matters to you."[7] Based on research by Kendall Bronk and colleagues, Suttie goes on to identify these seven ways to find purpose in life:

- Identify things you care about.
- Reflect on what matters most.
- Recognize your strengths and talents.
- Try volunteering.
- Imagine your best possible self.
- Cultivate positive emotions like gratitude and awe.
- Look to people you admire.[8]

Drawing on five decades of teaching and research, social psychologist Philip Zimbardo points to these seven paths to a meaningful and fulfilling life, one characterized by personal happiness and collective wellbeing:[9]

---

6. See Van Tongeren and Burnette, "Do You Believe Happiness Can Change?," 101–9.
7. See Suttie, "Seven Ways to Find."
8. Suttie, "Seven Ways to Find."
9. See Zimbardo, "Seven Paths to a Meaningful Life."

What Makes Our Relationships Meaningful, Fulfilling, and Satisfying?

- Use time wisely and well—be available for family, friends, and personal fun.
- Love a lifetime of learning—be filled with curiosity and wonder, asking why, discovering how, challenging ignorance, and demanding evidence for all assertions.
- Nurture passions—make passions an essential focus and energy source in life.
- Transform shyness into social engagement.
- Remake your image—take calculated risks, learn from mistakes, try harder and think wiser.
- Become a positive deviant—overcome the pressure of negative social norms with an inner sense of power of the one over the many.
- Train yourself to become an everyday hero—use compassion and empathy to become a willing social change agent daily.

Following psychiatrist and Holocaust survivor Viktor Frankl's notion that the search for meaning is the primary motivation in human beings, researcher and lecturer Pninit Russo-Netzer suggests that we "prioritize meaning." We can seek meaningful experiences in everyday life. Rather than simply wishing or hoping for a meaningful life, we can take ownership of cultivating and experiencing a meaningful life on a day-to-day basis. She notes, "People who are searching for meaning have a higher sense of meaning and wellbeing when they are actually prioritizing meaning in their daily lives."[10] As mentioned earlier, happiness can be fleeting. So, rather than enhance wellbeing through obsessing about happiness, Russo-Netzer suggests that we "prioritize positivity" by seeking out and scheduling our day around pleasant experiences. In other words, we control our actions rather than our feelings. While prioritizing meaning and positivity have many of the same wellbeing benefits, they differ in that people who prioritize meaning have a greater sense of meaning and gratitude while those prioritizing

---

10. See Russo-Netzer, "Why You Should Prioritize."

What Makes Our Relationships Meaningful, Satisfying, or Fulfilling?

positivity are less depressed. As Russo-Netzer wisely suggests, "Combining both strategies of prioritizing positivity and meaning may be the best approach. It could lead to short-term benefits, like happiness and positive feelings, as well as long-term benefits, like an overall sense of coherence in life."[11]

Steger and Russo-Netzer suggest that understanding and using our character strengths is another excellent way to cultivate meaning in our lives.

The study of character has a long history. In fact, in the early 2000s, fifty-five distinguished scientists spent three years seeking a set of virtues that reflect the complexity of human goodness which philosophy, ethics, and religion have in common. Beginning with Buddhist traditions 2,600 years ago, continuing with the traditions of Athenian philosophy, Confucianism, Taoism, Hinduism, Christianity, Judaism, and Islam, and reaching all the way to modern times, a list of six universal themes (virtues) was established: wisdom, courage, humanity, justice, temperance, and transcendence.[12] Character is viewed as positive qualities of our personality that people respect and admire. And character strengths "are personality traits that reflect our basic identity, produce positive outcomes for ourselves and others, and contribute to the collective good."[13] They are the central mechanisms that allow such other strengths to operate as our talents or abilities, interests or passions, skills or competencies, resources, and values. And they are routes to activate or express the six virtues. From research sponsored by the VIA Institute on Character, a VIA Classification of twenty-four positive personality characteristics ("character") was created to provide a common language for understanding what the best qualities in human beings are. Included in these pathways to the great virtues are the following twenty-four character strengths:[14]

---

11. Russo-Netzer, "Why You Should Prioritize."
12. See Peterson and Seligman, *Character Strengths and Virtues*.
13. See Niemiec and Pearce, "Practice of Character Strengths."
14. See Peterson and Seligman, *Character Strengths and Virtues*, 29–30.

What Makes Our Relationships Meaningful, Fulfilling, and Satisfying?

- Wisdom and Knowledge—cognitive strengths that entail the acquisition and use of knowledge, including *creativity, curiosity, open-mindedness, love of learning,* and *perspective.*
- Courage—emotional strengths that involve the exercise of will to accomplish goals in the face of opposition, external or internal, including *bravery, persistence, integrity,* and *vitality.*
- Humanity—interpersonal strengths that involve tending and befriending others, including *love, kindness,* and *social intelligence.*
- Justice—civic strengths that underlie healthy community life, including *citizenship, fairness,* and *leadership.*
- Temperance—strengths that protect against excess, including *forgiveness and mercy, humility, prudence,* and *self-regulation.*
- Transcendence—strengths that forge connections to the larger universe and provide meaning, including *appreciation of beauty and excellence, gratitude, hope, humor,* and *spirituality.*

The VIA Institute on Character is a nonprofit organization whose mission is to advance the science and practice of character strengths. Its signature VIA Survey is the only free scientific survey of character strengths in the world. Taken by more than 35 million people, this ten-minute online survey generates an individual character strengths profile featuring a top five list of character strengths, including one "signature" strength. For example, my signature strength is honesty,[15] followed by self-regulation,

---

15. Here's the way the website describes honesty: when you are honest, you speak the truth. More broadly, you present yourself in a genuine and sincere way, without pretense, and taking responsibility for your feelings and actions. You are a person of integrity—you are who you say you are—and you act consistently across the domains of your life rather than being one way in a community and a completely different way in your family. As a result, you believe you are being consistently true to yourself. This strength involves accurately representing your internal states, intentions, and commitments, both publicly and privately. The strength of honesty is often linked to self-concordance—the extent to which your goals accurately represent your implicit interests and values. Honesty allows people to take responsibility for their feelings and

What Makes Our Relationships Meaningful, Satisfying, or Fulfilling?

spirituality, creativity, and perseverance. People can learn to put their strengths into action with the following easy-to-learn, four-step, research-backed program:[16]

- Recognizing and appreciating strengths in others
- Exploring and using your signature strengths
- Applying your strengths to life challenges
- Making strengths a habit

To date, well over one thousand scientific and scholarly articles have been published on the VIA Classification, VIA Survey, or character strengths. And articles are posted on the VIA Institute website (https://www.viacharacter.org). For example, articles on relationships include building stronger relationships, connecting from a distance, dealing with difficult people, building compassionate communities, and committing to justice, equity, diversity, and inclusion. Moreover, there is an official guidebook from the VIA Institute on Character, *The Power of Character Strengths: Appreciate and Ignite Your Positive Personality* (2019), written by chief science and education officer Ryan M. Niemiec and senior scientist Robert E. McGrath. Niemiec has also authored the handbook *Character Strengths Interventions: A Field Guide for Practitioners* (2017).

An email from the VIA Institute poses this question: "Why do character strengths matter?" And the answer: "Your character strengths are the foundation of your true self. When you tune into and use your strengths, it's like having a superpower for building stronger connections and creating meaningful relationships. Strengths can even be used to set and achieve important goals, bringing increased motivation, resilience, and a hefty dose of accomplishments—which feel great!"[17]

---

behaviors, owning them, and reaping benefits by doing so. See VIA Institute on Character, "Honesty."

16. See Niemiec and McGrath, *Power of Character Strengths*, 275–98.

17. Email from VIA Institute on Character, "How Do Character Strengths Improve Happiness?"

What Makes Our Relationships Meaningful, Fulfilling, and Satisfying?

The VIA Institute website identifies additional ways character matters besides creating meaningful relationships, including:

- Boosting confidence
- Increasing happiness
- Strengthening relationships
- Managing problems
- Reducing stress
- Accomplishing goals
- Building meaning and purpose
- Improving work performance

Steger and Russo-Netzer point out that all twenty-four character strengths have a significant correlation with creating meaning in life. For example, research finds that perspective, love, spirituality, zest, and hope have strong correlations with meaningful living.[18] They also suggest ways that character strengths create significance, purpose, and coherence. They point out, for example, that "you can use your character strength of social intelligence to validate another person's sense of Significance, use your character strength of curiosity to uncover your Purpose and the courage to act upon it, or use your character strengths of perspective and wisdom to make sense of your life's story, memories, and experiences to develop more Coherence."[19]

Research on the role character strengths play in mental health finds that heart strengths (e.g., zest, gratitude, hope, love, curiosity, spirituality, humor, appreciation of beauty and excellence, social intelligence, kindness, forgiveness, teamwork, and leadership) are bridges to a fulfilling life and wellbeing more than mind strengths (e.g., love of learning, creativity, bravery, perspective, perseverance, self-regulation, fairness, modesty, honesty, prudence, and judgment). In fact, "according to the available literature, certain heart strengths (i.e., hope, zest, gratitude, love, and curiosity)

18. See Steger and Russo-Netzer, "To Have Your Best Life."
19. See Steger and Russo-Netzer, "To Have Your Best Life."

What Makes Our Relationships Meaningful, Satisfying, or Fulfilling?

help preserve relationships and are generally more closely related to subjective wellbeing than mind strengths, which are more individualistic."[20]

So, character matters! And as we'll see in chapter 2, signs of relational health and satisfaction include character as one of the Four C's in terms of the way we treat one another. We will also use our character strengths to create meaningful, satisfying, and fulfilling relationships in chapter 4.

Fulfilling Relationships

American psychologist and educator Martin Seligman, a pioneer in the field of positive psychology, makes an important distinction between happiness and flourishing. In fact, in his landmark book *Flourish: Visionary New Understanding of Happiness and Well-Being*, he describes how he changed his mind about authentic happiness theory and developed what he calls well-being theory. Here is how he explains this shift:[21]

> I used to think that the topic of positive psychology was happiness, that the gold standard for measuring happiness was life satisfaction, and that the goal of positive psychology was to increase life satisfaction. I now think that the topic of positive psychology is well-being, that the gold standard for measuring well-being is flourishing, and that the goal of positive psychology is to increase flourishing. This theory, which I call well-being theory, is very different from authentic happiness theory.

Seligman points to three inadequacies of authentic happiness theory. First, it centers on being in a cheerful mood, and as such does not account for such elements as engagement and meaning. Second, its goal, life satisfaction, is disproportionately tied to mood and determined by how good we feel at a particular moment. And third, it doesn't account for other essential elements

---

20. See Blasco-Belled, "Character Strengths and Mental Health," 25832–42.
21. Seligman, *Flourish*, 13.

What Makes Our Relationships Meaningful, Fulfilling, and Satisfying?

of life satisfaction. So, Seligman suggests that we center on the construct of wellbeing rather than the feeling of happiness, that our goal is to increase flourishing rather than life satisfaction, and that rather than measure life satisfaction, we measure these five elements of flourishing: positive emotion, engagement, meaning, positive relationships, and accomplishment (PERMA). Each element contributes to wellbeing, is pursued for its own sake, and is defined and measured independently of the other elements.

Positive emotion refers to the pleasant life, wherein happiness and life satisfaction are no longer the entire theory—rather they are one of the factors of positive emotion. Other positive emotions include hope, joy, love, compassion, pride, interest, gratitude, and amusement. A PERMA-Profiler measures how often people feel joyful, positive, and contented.[22]

Engagement is living in the present moment, focusing on the task at hand, and getting caught up in activities we love. The Profiler measures how often people are absorbed in what they are doing, lose track of time while doing something they enjoy, and are excited about and interested in things they enjoy.[23]

Positive relationships acknowledge we are social creatures, include interactions we have with others, and refer to feeling supported, valued, and loved by others. While the centrality of relationships to human welfare and flourishing is now commonly accepted by relationship science scholars,[24] positive relationships with others is a core element of mental health and wellbeing.[25] The Profiler measures the extent to which people feel loved, receive help and support from others when they need it, and are satisfied with their personal relationships.[26] Research on characteristics of close, meaningful, satisfying, supportive, and important

---

22. See Butler and Kern, "PERMA-Profiler," 14.

23. See Butler and Kern, "PERMA-Profiler," 14.

24. See appendix 1 for an overview of the academic field of relationship science.

25. See Caughlin and Huston, "Flourishing Literature on Flourishing Relationships," 25–35.

26. See Butler and Kern, "PERMA-Profiler," 14.

What Makes Our Relationships Meaningful, Satisfying, or Fulfilling? relationships identifies these four factors of positive relationships: self-improvement, practical support, emotional support, and shared enjoyment.[27]

Meaning has to do with our purpose in life and our sense of value and worth. It involves belonging to and serving something bigger than ourselves. Connections to other people and relationships are what give meaning and purpose to life. The Profiler measures the extent people lead a purposeful and meaningful life, feel that what they do in life is valuable and worthwhile, and generally feel they have a sense of direction in life.[28]

Accomplishments refer to our achievements, mastery, or competence. Flourishing and wellbeing occur when accomplishment comes from an internal motivation or striving just for the sake of the pursuit and improvement. The Profiler measures how often people achieve important goals they have set, handle their responsibilities, and make progress towards accomplishing their goals.[29]

Research demonstrates that people with high levels of wellbeing have these benefits compared to people with low wellbeing:[30]

- Perform better at work
- Have more satisfying relationships
- Are more cooperative
- Have stronger immune systems
- Have better physical health
- Live longer
- Have reduced cardiovascular mortality
- Have fewer sleep problems
- Have lower level of burnout
- Have greater self-control

27. See Paschalia et al., "Positive Relationships Questionnaire (PRQ)," 1039–57.
28. See Butler and Kern, "PERMA-Profiler," 14.
29. See Butler and Kern, "PERMA-Profiler," 15.
30. See Positive Psychology Center, "PERMA Theory of Well-Being."

What Makes Our Relationships Meaningful, Fulfilling, and Satisfying?
- Have better self-regulation and coping abilities
- Are more prosocial

Moreover, research identifies optimism as a key wellbeing contributor with many benefits compared to pessimism, including:[31]

- Less depression and anxiety
- Better performance
- Reduced risk of dropping out of school
- Better physical health outcomes, including fewer reported illnesses, less coronary heart disease, lower mortality risk, and faster recovery from surgery

The science of wellbeing also identifies these important implications for institutional applications:[32]

- Wellbeing skills can be taught, so schools can educate students for flourishing as well as for workplace success.
- Parents can cultivate their children's strengths, grit, and resilience.
- Workplaces can improve performance as well as raise employee wellbeing.
- Therapists can nurture their patients' strengths to prevent mental illness, enhance flourishing, and heal damage.
- Communities can encourage public service and civic engagement.

For Seligman, positive psychology links fulfillment with both satisfaction and meaning.

He puts it this way:

> Positive Psychology takes seriously the bright hope that if you find yourself stuck in the parking lot of life, with

---

31. Positive Psychology Center, "PERMA Theory of Well-Being."
32. Positive Psychology Center, "PERMA Theory of Well-Being."

What Makes Our Relationships Meaningful, Satisfying, or Fulfilling?

few and only ephemeral pleasures, with minimal gratifications, and without meaning, there is a road out. This road takes you through the countryside of pleasure and gratification, up into the high country of strength and virtue, and finally to the peaks of lasting fulfillment: meaning and purpose.[33]

Put another way, "according to Seligman's research, he believes that the PERMA Model's five core elements are what people need in order to achieve a healthy sense of wellbeing, fulfillment, and satisfaction in life that can lead to finding life's true meaning."[34]

Satisfying Relationships

Interest in the topic of relationship satisfaction in a variety of disciplines such as communication, psychology, sociology, and family studies focuses on one type of relationship: romantic relationships in general, and married couples in particular. In research on couples, for example, "relationship satisfaction is widely viewed as the final common pathway that leads to relationship breakdown. . . . Not surprisingly, relationship satisfaction is the gold standard for evaluating interventions designed to alleviate relationship distress."[35] Perhaps more importantly, studies on relationship satisfaction "focus almost exclusively on Western—and, more particularly, North American—relationships. Moreover, with a few exceptions, most of the assessment devices used to study relationship satisfaction have focused on one particular relationship: marriage."[36] The study of close relationships from social, clinical, and counseling psychology also explores a range of theoretical and clinical approaches to understand and promote relationship satisfaction—in intimate and love relationships.[37]

---

33. Seligman, *Authentic Happiness*, xiv.
34. See CFI Team, "What Is the PERMA Model?"
35. Fincham et al., "Relationship Satisfaction," 422.
36. Fincham et al., "Relationship Satisfaction," 423.
37. See Sternberg and Hojjat, *Satisfaction in Close Relationships*.

What Makes Our Relationships Meaningful, Fulfilling, and Satisfying?

In sum, despite this plethora of relationship satisfaction research and publication by relationship and social scientists, the primary interest in relationship satisfaction focuses on married couples. And most measurement instruments for relationship satisfaction are constructed to measure whether or not married couples are satisfied with their relationships.[38] Predictors or determinants of relational satisfaction are yet to be discovered, particularly for close personal relationships in general. A literature review of such inventories finds two instruments that measure whether or not people's relationships in general are satisfying: the Burns Relationship Satisfaction Scale (RSAT) and Wright Acquaintance Description Form-F2 (ADF-F2).

Psychiatrist David D. Burns created the seven-item RSAT in 1983 with categories to measure overall relationship satisfaction in close relationships including communication and openness, resolving conflicts and arguments, degree of affection and caring, intimacy and closeness, and satisfaction with roles.[39]

Psychologist Paul H. Wright created the seventy-item ADF-F2 in 1985 with scales to measure fourteen characteristics of friendship relationships including relationship strength (voluntary interdependence and person-qua-person), relationship values (utility, stimulation, ego support, self-affirmation, and security), tension/strain (maintenance difficulty-personal and maintenance difficulty-situational), relationship differentiation (exclusiveness, permanence, emotional expression, and social regulation), and relationship bias (general favorability).[40]

Our interest in relationship satisfaction in this study is more with close personal relationships in general than with intimate relationships such as marriage in particular. Moreover, we will be

---

38. For a review of these relationship satisfaction measures see Graham et al., "Reliability of Relationship Satisfaction," 39–48; Funk and Rogge, "Testing the Ruler," 572–83; and Hendrick, "Generic Measure of Relationship Satisfaction," 91–98.

39. See Burns, *Feeling Good Together*, 41–42. See also Burns, *Ten Days to Self-Esteem*.

40. See Wright, "Bare-Bones Guide." See also Wright, "Acquaintance Description Form," 39–62.

What Makes Our Relationships Meaningful, Satisfying, or Fulfilling?

interested less in the relationship satisfaction of married couples than with identifying factors or qualities that cause or create satisfying relationships in the first place. Likewise, our interest is more with determinants or predictors of satisfaction in close personal relationships than with whether or not love relationships are satisfying. Later, in chapters 2 and 3, we'll examine four qualities of relationship satisfaction and twelve guidelines for relational health and satisfaction, together with measures of these predictors of relationship satisfaction.

In the field of interpersonal relationships, features of satisfying relationships have been derived from more than seven hundred articles and books by speech communication scholar Julia Wood. In fact, she identifies four essential dimensions of satisfying interpersonal relationships: investment, commitment, trust, and comfort with relational dialectics.[41] For friendship relationships, in particular, Wood identifies these five dimensions: willing to invest, emotional closeness, acceptance, trust, and support.[42] Even in romantic relationships, these dimensions of friendship relationships are vitally important. For example, empirical research finds that the friendship core of romantic relationships carries more weight than the sexual aspect of the relationships.[43]

Research by Therese Naslund and Sophia Reinholdsson examines features of relationship satisfaction in both friendship and romantic relationships.[44] Ninety-three university students ages eighteen to forty-one were asked to describe in their own words what is currently making them experience satisfaction, and why, in their friendship/romantic relationships. Thematic analysis of responses find that balance, similarities, communication, closeness, trust, understanding, safety, and conflict management are

---

41. See Wood, *Relational Communication*. See also a description of these four features of satisfying relationships in Wood's *Interpersonal Communication in Everyday Encounters*, 219–25.

42. Wood, *Interpersonal Communication in Everyday Encounters*, 283–88.

43. See VanderDrift et al., "Friendship and Romance," 109–22.

44. See Naslund and Reinholdsson, "Features Behind Relationship Satisfaction."

What Makes Our Relationships Meaningful, Fulfilling, and Satisfying?

satisfying features for both types of relationships. Support was also a theme for friendship relationships and hope for the future a feature of romantic relationships.

Several of these themes are among Wood's five dimensions, e.g., closeness, trust, and support, although acceptance and willing to invest are missing. Notably, passion, attraction, and sex are missing in both lists. Moreover, as we'll see in chapter 2, most of these themes are similar to some of this study's ten themes of meaningful, satisfying, and fulfilling relationships. For example, trust, closeness, and support are similar to connection; balance and similarities are similar to mutuality; safety and understanding are related to being oneself/known; conflict management part of work; and communication a feature of both lists.[45]

And then research by psychologists Louise C. Hawkley and John T. Cacioppo on social connectedness and relationship satisfaction concludes that middle-aged and older adults in an urban setting find comfort, solace, and security in relationships with individuals, groups, pets, and deities.[46] These three dimensions of

---

45. Two additional notions of healthy relationships should be noted. The first is Buddhist psychotherapist David Richo's five keys that open us to meaningful, fulfilling, and intimate relationships, including: being attentive (instead of ignoring, refusing to listen, being unavoidable, or fearing the truth), being accepting (rather than trying to make someone over to fit our specifications, desires, or fantasies), being appreciative (instead of criticizing), being affectionate (instead of acting selfishly or abusively), and allowing (rather than being controlling, demanding, or manipulative). Viewed in spiritual terms, these five keys can be understood as follows: attention means consciousness of the interconnectedness of all things; acceptance means affirming an unconditional yes to the sobering givens of existence, the facts of life; appreciation means the attitude of gratitude; affection means the love we feel for others and for the universe; and allowing means that we grant to others and protect in ourselves the right to live free and without outside control. See *How to Be an Adult in Relationships*, 52–53. The second perspective on healthy relationships is the five agreements of Toltec wisdom we make with ourselves, other people, God, and life to experience freedom, happiness, and authenticity, including: be impeccable with your word, don't take anything personally, don't make assumptions, always do your best, and be skeptical but learn to listen. See Ruiz, et al, *The Fifth Agreement*.

46. See Hawkley and Cacioppo, "How Can I Connect with Thee," 43–58.

What Makes Our Relationships Meaningful, Satisfying, or Fulfilling?

relationship satisfaction are similar to one of our four qualities, interpersonal security and warmth.

SUMMARY

Chapter 1 features learnings from three strands of social science research. First, we've learned from social scientists that meaningful relationships are ones that have significance, purpose, and coherence. Belonging, transcendence, and character strengths also create meaningful relationships. Ways character strengths create meaningful living include social intelligence for significance, curiosity and courage for purpose, and perspective and wisdom for coherence. Second, we've seen that fulfilling relationships are ones that bring wellbeing and flourishing. Elements of flourishing include positive emotion, engagement, meaning, positive relationships, and accomplishment. Heart character strengths such as hope, zest, gratitude, love, and curiosity help preserve relationships and are bridges to a fulfilling life and wellbeing. Moreover, fulfilling relationships are closely linked to meaningful and satisfying relationships. And third, we've discovered that satisfying relationships are ones with a broad array of features including communication and conflict management, closeness and support, trust and acceptance, balance and similarities, safety and caring, comfort and security, and investment and affection.[47]

PRACTICAL APPLICATIONS

Think of several personal relationships that are meaningful, satisfying, or fulfilling for you.

1. To what extent do these relationships have significance, purpose, and coherence for you?[48]

47. As a conclusion in chapter 4, we will create a new Relationship Satisfaction Inventory (RSI) to measure these features of satisfying relationships (see appendix 14).

48. For this and related questions, use a scale of 1 to 6 where 1 equals never

What Makes Our Relationships Meaningful, Fulfilling, and Satisfying?

2. How does the character strength of social intelligence give significance to these relationships? How do curiosity and courage give them purpose? How do perspective and wisdom give them coherence?
3. To what extent are you understood, recognized, valued, and affirmed?
4. To what extent do you experience a sense of belonging and connection?
5. To what extent do they fill you with awe or wonder? How about help you rise above the everyday world to experience a higher reality?
6. To what extent do these relationships bring you wellbeing or flourishing?
7. How often do you feel joyful, positive, and contented?
8. To what extent do you feel loved, receive emotional and practical support, and feel satisfied with these personal relationships?
9. How often do you engage in the present moment, focus on the task at hand, or get caught up in activities you love in these relationships?
10. How do such character strengths as hope, zest, gratitude, love, spirituality, humor, kindness, and forgiveness help maintain your relationships and provide bridges to a fulfilling life and wellbeing?
11. To what extent are you satisfied with your communication and conflict management? Closeness and support? Trust and acceptance? Balance and similarities? Safety and caring? Investment and affection?

---

or very little and 6 equals always or very much.

2

What Makes Our Relationships Meaningful, Satisfying, or Fulfilling?

ANSWERS FROM ORDINARY PEOPLE

WHEN I BEGAN GRADUATE studies in 1975, I brought with me this question: What makes our relationships meaningful, satisfying, or fulfilling? And I conducted a research project with ordinary people focused on this question. In 1975, the study of interpersonal communication and the field of relationship science were in their infancy. Moreover, the topic of relationship satisfaction was of limited interest to social and behavioral scientists.[1] And a review of the scant literature on relationship satisfaction concluded: "In sum, since no theoretical formulation adequately explains the construct of relationship satisfaction, since no adequate measure is available for the attitude, and since no emphasis on the interaction between persons in relationship is to be found, the task of empirically developing an Interpersonal Relationship Satisfaction Inventory was undertaken. It is hoped that this research will provide

---

1. As we'll see later, the primary interest in relationship satisfaction centered on married couples.

What Makes Our Relationships Meaningful, Satisfying, or Fulfilling?

communication researchers and other social scientists with a useful measure of interpersonal relationship satisfaction and with relevant variables which further its theoretical understanding."[2]

Research Project—1975

The original research project seeks to further our understanding and measurement of meaningful, satisfying, or fulfilling relationships. For a summary of this research, see appendix 2. Using ordinary people as subjects, four qualities of meaningful, satisfying, or fulfilling relationships emerge: *communication openness, being oneself, interpersonal security and warmth,* and *personal support and growth*. And a forty-item Interpersonal Relationship Satisfaction Inventory (IRSA) was developed to measure meaningful, satisfying, or fulfilling relationships (see appendix 3).[3]

Results of this original study, then, discover that the construct meaningful, satisfying, or fulfilling relationships is multidimensional in nature. While four factors are clearly discernible, the relationship among them is not yet clear. Moreover, the four qualities that surface in the empirically developed inventory are in accord with no particular then-current theory of interpersonal relationship satisfaction. This lack of theoretical clarity is perhaps understandable since no theory at that time viewed relationship satisfaction as an attitude per se, nor had one emphasized the relational interaction itself. However, since elements from previous

2. See Kirkpatrick, "Conceptualizing and Measuring Relationship Satisfaction," 8–9.

3. A twelve-item valid and reliable short form of the Interpersonal Relationship Satisfaction Inventory was also developed identifying these four factors: *openness, acceptance, warmth, and support and growth* (see appendix 4). I used this twelve-item short-form version as a measure of meaningful and satisfying close personal relationships in my 1978 DMin dissertation research, "Conceptualizing and Developing Community in a Congregation." See appendix A, "Final Questionnaire Form," 125–42. It measured the extent to which a respondent's close personal relationships as a whole are meaningful and satisfying. Close personal relationships are considered to be "good friends," wherein good friends are distinct from four other types of interpersonal relationships: strangers, acquaintances, friends, and intimates.

21

What Makes Our Relationships Meaningful, Satisfying, or Fulfilling?

social and behavioral science research such as growth, need, and social climate, etc.,[4] are related to the factors that emerge in this study, a new eclectic theory is likely to evolve from the findings of this study and future research.

The conclusion of this research project conducted fifty years ago includes this aspiration and suggestion for further research: "While the present investigation finds relationship satisfaction to be a multidimensional construct, a promising direction for future research is to determine the relationship among components."[5]

Research Project—2025

Guidelines for Relational Health and Satisfaction

Picking up where the research from 1975 left off—namely to explore the relationship among the four qualities of meaningful, satisfying, or fulfilling relationships (openness, acceptance, warmth, and growth)—I recently created a system of relational communication ethics based on these four *qualities* with the goal of *relational health and satisfaction* using the following *guidelines*:[6]

- Guidelines for openness: sharing, risking, and assertiveness
- Guidelines for acceptance: listening, trusting, and empathy
- Guidelines for warmth: caring, connecting, and mutuality
- Guidelines for growth: supporting, empowering, and curiosity

---

4. See, for example, the need-orientations of Maslow, Alderfer, and Schultz; Heslin and Dunphy's focus on small group member participation; Moos's focus on group social climate; Wright's friendship model; Barrett-Lennard's Rogerian-based growth orientation; and Frankl's meaning orientation. For more information on these social and behavioral scientists' relationship-satisfaction-related conceptualizations, see Kirkpatrick, "Conceptualizing and Measuring Relationship Satisfaction," 4–10.

5. Kirkpatrick, "Conceptualizing and Measuring Relationship Satisfaction," 16.

6. See Kirkpatrick, *Communication in the Church*, 122.

What Makes Our Relationships Meaningful, Satisfying, or Fulfilling?

Elsewhere, I summarize these four foundational or underlying qualities and components of relational health and satisfaction as follows: "Openness leads to the freedom and safety to share those things in our personal lives that matter most. Acceptance means that what we share is treated with respect, nonjudgmentally, and reverently as on holy ground. Warmth refers to a quality or feeling of intimacy, appreciation, and affection. Finally, growth is fostered through a curiosity that sparks a desire to learn, and through the support and empowerment necessary for actualizing our God-given human potential."[7] Indeed, these four qualities have the power to transform our relationships by making them meaningful, satisfying, or fulfilling. Therefore, these four qualities may be considered determinants or predictors of meaningful, satisfying, or fulfilling relationships.[8]

Four C's Approach to Relational Health

Thus far, we've been considering relational health and satisfaction in interpersonal relationships. Elsewhere I've introduced a Four C's approach to relational health in organizations, using traces of these guidelines as signs of relational health centered in *community, communication, character,* and *collaboration.* Community has to do with *ways we share with one another,* communication with *ways we interact with one another,* character with *ways we treat one another,* and collaboration with *ways we work with one another.* Twenty-four practical ways these four signs of relational health are exemplified are drawn from the latest relational and social science empirical research (see appendix 5).[9]

To further explore the relationship among our four qualities of meaningful, satisfying, or fulfilling relationships, a new research project was designed with the following hypotheses, participants, results, observations and discussion, and conclusions.

7. See Kirkpatrick, *Signs of Hope and Health,* 54.
8. I also refer to these four factors as signs of healthy relationships.
9. See Kirkpatrick, *Signs of Hope and Health,* 54–74, including a synopsis of practical ways each of the twenty-four signs is exemplified.

What Makes Our Relationships Meaningful, Satisfying, or Fulfilling?

Hypotheses

1. Participants in this current research project will replicate the finding from fifty years ago that what makes relationships meaningful, satisfying, or fulfilling are communication openness (openness); being oneself (acceptance); interpersonal security and warmth (warmth); and personal support and growth (growth).
2. Responses to the research question will reveal a fit between relational health and satisfaction and the twelve guidelines for openness, acceptance, warmth, and growth.
3. Responses to the research question will reveal a fit between the Four C's as signs of relational health, including the six ways each is demonstrated, and the themes and components of meaningful, satisfying, or fulfilling relationships that emerge.

Participants (Email and Text Contacts)

One hundred ninety-one ordinary people were contacted and asked for one or two (or more) brief responses to the research question: What makes your relationship (with people) meaningful, satisfying, or fulfilling? Participants were recruited from my family members, friends, good friends, and colleagues.[10]

Participants range in age from eight to ninety-three. Family members are predominantly Caucasian; politically and religiously diverse; professional and middle class; and college educated.

10. Included are 56 family members (1 spouse, 13 children and in-laws, 9 siblings and spouses, 5 cousins, 13 nieces and nephews, and 15 grandchildren); 49 friends (10 neighbors, 13 current Rainier Beach Presbyterian Church parishioners, 6 former Galena Westminster United Presbyterian Church parishioners, 16 former Kent First Presbyterian Church parishioners, and 4 family friends); 14 good friends (note: 30 family members and 4 colleagues are also good friends); and 72 colleagues (42 clergypersons and 30 laypersons with whom I have worked, mainly in Olympia Presbytery of the PCUSA) (note: 5 family members are also clergypersons).

What Makes Our Relationships Meaningful, Satisfying, or Fulfilling?

Friends and good friends are also predominantly Caucasian; tend to be progressive politically and religiously; are professional and middle class; and college educated. Colleagues are typically progressive Presbyterian clergy and laypersons, including some diversity among racial ethnic, sexual orientation, and gender identity demographics. While including a sizable number of privileged participants, most live into Pulitzer Prize-winning American journalist Isabel Wilkerson's admonition in *Caste: The Origins of Our Discontents*: "The price of privilege is the moral duty to act when one sees another person treated unfairly. And the least that a person in the dominant caste can do is not make the pain any worse."[11]

Everyone was contacted by email except neighbors and grandchildren. Neighbors and grandchildren were contacted by text message since that is my primary means of electronic communication with them.

Results

Participant responses typically include the following: "That's a great question." "It is thought-provoking." "Thank you for asking." "Here's my response." And "I hope it is helpful." Responses range from one word to 783 words. Here's my typical response: "Thank you for your thoughtful, insightful, and personal response to my research question—just what I am looking and hoping for. I really appreciate you taking the time to reflect and respond! With gratitude, Tom."

Participant responses were examined verbatim for purposes of data analysis, hypothesis testing, and inventory development. Overall, 126 of 191 people responded to the research question. This 66 percent return rate includes 41 of 56 family members (73 percent), 31 of 49 friends (63 percent), 9 of 14 good friends (64 percent), and 45 of 72 colleagues (63 percent).

A content analysis of participant responses generated these ten themes of meaningful, satisfying, or fulfilling relationships:

11. Wilkerson, *Caste*, 386.

What Makes Our Relationships Meaningful, Satisfying, or Fulfilling?

connection, mutuality, enjoyment, communication, time, being oneself/known, growth, work, presence, and transcendence.[12]

In order to identify components or descriptors for each theme, closer analysis of participant responses generated the frequency of theme-related word usage (see appendix 7).

Next, components for each theme were selected from these commonly used words and phrases by respondents, resulting in descriptions for each theme (see appendix 8).

Observations and Discussion

Hypothesis 1

Hypothesis 1 predicts that participants in this current research project will replicate the finding from fifty years ago that what makes relationships meaningful, satisfying, or fulfilling are communication openness (openness); being oneself (acceptance); interpersonal security and warmth (warmth); and personal support and growth (growth).

Three of the original findings are replicated: communication openness, being oneself, and personal support and growth. Whereas the fourth, interpersonal security and warmth, has some resemblance to the new theme of enjoyment (e.g., affection, comfort, hugs, positivity, and camaraderie), neither the words "security" nor "warmth" are used in any participant's response. And besides communication, being oneself, growth, and enjoyment, six additional themes of meaningful, satisfying, or fulfilling relationships are identified in the new research: connection, mutuality, time, work, presence, and transcendence. Remember, though, that the original four qualities of relationship satisfaction were limited statistically by a four-factor solution using factor analysis. In any event, our new research provides a more robust and rich array of ten themes, seven of which are new.

---

12. On average, participant responses include three of the ten themes (397 theme-related responses from 126 respondents). For the number and percentage of participants that include each theme in their responses, see appendix 6.

What Makes Our Relationships Meaningful, Satisfying, or Fulfilling?

Hypothesis 2

This hypothesis predicts that responses to the research question will reveal a fit between the ways relationships are meaningful, satisfying, or fulfilling and the twelve guidelines for openness, acceptance, growth, and warmth.

Again, results are mixed. For example, two of the three guidelines for communication openness are found among the components of the new communication theme (sharing and risking), while the third, assertiveness, is missing. Moreover, many additional descriptors appear in the communication theme (e.g., listening, honesty, empathy, and truthfulness, along with electronic and nonverbal communication).

Next, whereas trusting and empathy appear in both the guidelines for acceptance and the theme of being oneself/known, listening is missing. And, again, there are many additional components of being oneself/known, such as courage, genuineness, safe space, integrity, affirmation, vulnerable, and patience.

And while supporting and empowering are present in both the guidelines and components of growth, curiosity is missing as a component of growth. As before, there are many additional components of growth such as accountability, openness to change, courage, humility, practicing forgiveness, and navigating obstacles.

Finally, whereas warmth per se is missing as a theme, it is intriguing that two themes, connection and mutuality, both appear as guidelines for warmth. Perhaps there are more similarities between the two than first appears.

In sum, two of three guidelines for openness, acceptance, growth, and warmth are present as components in the themes of communication, being oneself, and growth, and as themes of connection and mutuality. In addition, five new themes of meaningful, satisfying, or fulfilling relationships are identified: enjoyment, time, work, presence, transcendence.

What Makes Our Relationships Meaningful, Satisfying, or Fulfilling?

Hypothesis 3

This hypothesis expects responses to the research question will reveal a fit between the Four C's as signs of relational health, including the six ways each is demonstrated, and the emergent themes and components of meaningful, satisfying, or fulfilling relationships.

At first glance, results identify only one of the Four C's, communication, among our ten themes of meaningful, satisfying, or fulfilling relationships. And a comparison of the six ways communication is expressed with the new components of communication reveal mixed results. Listening and technological savvy appear on both lists whereas appreciation is a component of being oneself/known, common ground of connection, and engaging conflict of work. Curiosity does not appear as a component of any theme.

A closer examination, however, finds striking similarities between ways the other three C's (community, character, and collaboration) are exhibited and the thematic components of connection and growth. For instance, five of six ways community is exemplified are present as components of connection, including building relationships, supporting, trust, empathy, and bridging cultures— only forgiveness is missing, although it appears as a component of both growth and work. Moreover, four of six ways character is expressed—kindness, humility, compassion, and love— are also components of connection (peace and justice are each cited once by the same participant). And whereas openness to change and engaging gifts as ways to collaborate are also components of growth, each of the other four ways to collaborate are related to growth (strategizing and visioning, discerning and decision-making, organizational agility, and partnering).

After further and more thorough analysis, then, there is a remarkable fit between all four C's and three of the ten themes. *Communication* is present in both lists, although ways to communicate and components of communication have modest overlap. It is noteworthy, though, to find most ways both *community* and *character* are demonstrated among components of the theme

What Makes Our Relationships Meaningful, Satisfying, or Fulfilling?

connection. Likewise, ways to *collaborate* are remarkably similar to components of *growth*. We should keep in mind, however, that while there's a fit between the Four C's of relational health and satisfaction and the themes of communication, connection, and growth, there are seven additional themes and distinctive ways participants in this study find their relationships to be meaningful, satisfying, or fulfilling.[13]

CONCLUSIONS

1. Results from this research project based on responses from ordinary people replicate three of the four qualities of relationship satisfaction identified fifty years ago—communication (openness), being oneself (acceptance), and growth. They also reveal a fit between two of three guidelines for each of our four qualities of relationship health and satisfaction, and the components of communication, being oneself, growth, and the themes of connection and mutuality. Moreover, there is a fit for ways each of the Four C's are demonstrated and the themes and components communication, connection, and growth.

2. Results from the responses of "ordinary people" also advance our knowledge about ways our relationships are meaningful, satisfying, or fulfilling with our discovery of ten themes. In addition, many components are identified for each of our ten themes, including 29 for connection, 18 for mutuality, 23 for enjoyment, 16 for communication, 7 for time, 20 for being oneself/known, 23 for growth, 11 for work, 15 for presence, and 15 for transcendence. Note: in the follow-up research project presented in chapter 3, three descriptors for

13. For another research project, I created and administered Google Forms questionnaires to measure signs of hope and health in mainline churches reported by their denominational leaders and selected pastors. This research project includes measures of the Four C's, including the six ways each is demonstrated. For information about this project, see Kirkpatrick, *Signs of Hope and Health*.

What Makes Our Relationships Meaningful, Satisfying, or Fulfilling?

each theme will emerge from clusters of these component words and phrases and will be used to operationalize the ten themes in a new research questionnaire.

3. Responses from our "ordinary people" participants provide a basis to operationalize our ten themes by creating an inventory to measure meaningful, satisfying, and fulfilling (MSF) relationships for use by social science researchers, therapists, and individuals. This new *MSF Relationships Inventory* was created using brief one-sentence descriptions for each of the ten themes (see appendix 9). A six-point Likert scale may be used to assess both general or overall relationship meaningfulness, satisfaction, and fulfillment and theme-specific relationship meaningfulness, satisfaction, and fulfillment with whatever referent one selects, e.g., close personal relationships, couple relationships, etc., for initial testing. To date, the validity and reliability of this inventory has not been tested or assessed.

4. While working on this research project, I made a surprising and somewhat astounding discovery: I have a *meaningful* relationship with each of my 191 family members, friends, good friends, and colleagues. We've spent quality time together, enjoy each other's presence, are interested in one other's interests, respect and trust each other, appreciate each other's uniqueness, and make a positive impact on each other's lives and worlds. With colleagues we've done important work together and made significant contributions from our efforts. But are these relationships also *satisfying* and *fulfilling*? Well, not necessarily. In fact, I don't expect that my relationships with all of them will be either *satisfying* or *fulfilling*. I do find that my close personal relationships with good friends and with some family members, friends, and colleagues are *satisfying* and *fulfilling*. More will be said about these distinctions in the observations and discussion of the follow-up research project. For now, let's examine a

What Makes Our Relationships Meaningful, Satisfying, or Fulfilling?

little more closely what makes relationships *meaningful*, what makes them *satisfying*, and what makes them *fulfilling*.

One way to explore these four key words is to examine the frequency with which they are used by respondents in this study. For a frequency breakdown, see appendix 10.

As evident in appendix 10, the word "relationship(s)" is used an average of two times per participant in their responses. Next, notice that the word "meaningful" is used by nearly half of the participants, nearly twice as often as the words "satisfying" and "fulfilling"—although "meaningful" and "satisfying" are each used alone by around 15 percent of the participants. And you can see that all four words are used together by only 5 percent of participants. Finally, the words "meaningful," "satisfying," and "fulfilling" are not used very often with the word "relationship(s)," although "meaningful relationship(s)" appears much more frequently than either "satisfying relationship(s)" or "fulfilling relationship(s)."

It appears that participants in this study use the word "meaningful" more often than either "satisfying" or "fulfilling." However, I don't think this necessarily means that it is twice as important—after all, I list it first whenever I use the three in combination and participants may simply use it as shorthand for all three. It would not surprise me, though, that it stands out for participants, similarly as it does for me, as a more relevant descriptor for their relationships in general.

Another way to explore these three words is to consider their dictionary definitions and see if there are similarities and differences among them. Here are online definitions for each:

- *Meaningful*—having purpose or significance;[14] or having a serious, important, or useful quality or purpose[15]

---

14. Merriam-Webster, "Meaningful."
15. Oxford Learners Dictionaries, "Meaningful."

What Makes Our Relationships Meaningful, Satisfying, or Fulfilling?

- *Satisfying*—pleasure or contentment by providing what is needed or wanted; enjoyable, gratifying;[16] or giving fulfillment or the pleasure associated with this[17]
- *Fulfilling*—providing happiness or satisfaction;[18] or making someone satisfied or happy because of realizing their hopes or expectations, or fully developing their character or abilities[19]

"Meaningful," then, is a state of having *purpose or significance*, whereas "satisfying" and "fulfilling" are both feelings and are closely related. "Satisfying" is the feeling of *enjoyment, pleasure, or contentment* from fulfilling one's wants or desires, whereas "fulfilling" is the feeling of *happiness or satisfaction* from realizing one's hopes or expectations or fully developing their character or abilities.

So, while my relationships with all 191 ordinary people who participated in this study have purpose or significance, they may or may not bring enjoyment, pleasure, and contentment, or happiness and satisfaction. All are significant, whereas those with whom I have a close personal relationship also bring feelings of enjoyment, pleasure, or contentment, and feelings of happiness or satisfaction.

SUMMARY

As we'll see in chapter 3, after completing the 2025 research project, several new questions emerge along with a follow-up research project designed using the same collection of ordinary people as participants. And we will revisit the question of how best to define relationships that are "meaningful," "satisfying," or "fulfilling."

16. Merriam-Webster, "Satisfying."
17. Oxford English Dictionary, "Satisfying."
18. Merriam-Webster, "Fulfilling."
19. Oxford Learners Dictionaries, "Fulfilling."

What Makes Our Relationships Meaningful, Satisfying, or Fulfilling?

After considering the way ordinary people understand these three words and the way the dictionary defines them in this chapter, and being mindful of the more nuanced way social scientists define them in chapter 1, we will need a comprehensive yet succinct definition for each word in chapter 3. Here, then, are the eclectic, composite definitions we will use:

- A *meaningful* relationship is one having significance, value, or importance.
- A *satisfying* relationship is one bringing enjoyment, pleasure, or contentment.
- A *fulfilling* relationship is one that thrives or flourishes.

PRACTICAL APPLICATIONS

1. What are one or two (or more) brief responses to this question: What makes your relationships meaningful, satisfying, or fulfilling?
2. In your relationships as a whole, to what extent do you find them meaningful?[20]
3. In your relationships as a whole, to what extent do you find them satisfying? Assess your satisfaction with your close personal relationships using the Relationship Satisfaction Inventory in appendix 14. What do you learn about yourself and your relationships from your responses? Note: you can also assess your satisfaction with other types of relationships, e.g., personal, acquaintance, friendship, or intimate relationships.
4. In your relationships as a whole, to what extent do you find them fulfilling?

---

20. For this and related questions, use a scale of 1 to 6 where 1 equals never or very little and 6 equals always or very much.

What Makes Our Relationships Meaningful, Satisfying, or Fulfilling?

5. Assess the extent to which your relationships are meaningful, satisfying, or fulfilling in terms of the ten themes using the MSF Relationships Inventory in appendix 9. What do you learn about yourself and your relationships from your responses?

3

What Makes Our Relationships Meaningful, Satisfying, or Fulfilling?

ANSWERS FROM FOLLOW-UP RESEARCH PROJECT

AFTER COMPLETING THE 2025 research project, several new questions have emerged and a follow-up research project has been designed. Here are this project's research questions, questionnaire, hypotheses, results, observations and discussion, and conclusions.

Research Questions

First, how are respondents doing in their meaningful, satisfying, or fulfilling relationships with respect to their four relational health *qualities* and to their ten relational health *themes*? For example, to what extent can they be open in their communication, be themselves, experience interpersonal security and warmth, and experience personal support and growth? And to what extent do they connect with people; have mutual interests; enjoy being together; communicate well; spend time together; feel free to be themselves;

learn and grow; work at their relationships; are present and available to one another; and feed their souls and spirits?

In order to measure the extent to which respondents experience each of the four qualities and the ten themes, descriptors were created for each quality from the relational health and satisfaction guidelines and twelve-item Interpersonal Relationship Satisfaction Inventory (IRSI), and for each theme from clusters of component words and phrases.

Next, in asking these questions, how should the words "meaningful," "satisfying," and "fulfilling" be defined? And by whom—the respondents or myself? Respondents will be asked to define a meaningful/satisfying/fulfilling (hereafter m/s/f) relationship both in order to gain fresh insight about the meaning of each word and to learn what they mean to respondents as they answer the questions. In addition, each respondent will be asked the extent to which their m/s/f relationships "have significance, value or importance" (my composite definition for *meaningful* relationships), "bring enjoyment, pleasure, or contentment" (my composite definition for *satisfying* relationships), and "thrive or flourish" (my composite definition for *fulfilling* relationships).

Also, how many m/s/f relationships with people do they have? And among what types of personal relationships are most respondents' m/s/f relationships—family members, friends, good friends, colleagues, or a combination of these types of personal relationships?

And then, how do respondents rate the overall health of their m/s/f relationships?

Research Questionnaire

In order to answer these new research questions, Google Forms questionnaires were created. The original 191 "ordinary people" respondents were assigned to three equal groups, one-third receiving a Meaningful Relationships Questionnaire, one-third a Satisfying Relationships Questionnaire, and one-third a Fulfilling Relationships Questionnaire. An equal number of family

What Makes Our Relationships Meaningful, Satisfying, or Fulfilling?

members, friends, good friends, and colleagues received each of the three questionnaires. Each questionnaire includes the same questions, modified only by reference to their m/s/f relationships. See appendix 11 for the questionnaire questions.

Research Project Hypotheses[1]

1. We will gain fresh insights into the meanings of *meaningful* relationships, *satisfying* relationships, and *fulfilling* relationships (question 1).

2. Most respondents will have 4–10 or 10–30 m/s/f relationships. The number of respondents with meaningful relationships (question 2) will be substantially higher (30–60 or higher) than for respondents with either satisfying or fulfilling relationships (4–10 or 10–30). Few respondents will report having either very few relationships (3 or fewer) or very many relationships (100 or more).

3. Most m/s/f relationships will be among family members or good friends (question 3).

4. In their relationships as a whole, most respondents will rate the extent to which they find them m/s/f quite highly (5 or 6 on question 4).

5. Most respondents will rate the overall health of their m/s/f relationships quite highly (5 or 6 on question 5).

---

1. Except for hypothesis 2, which is based on my own experience, the hypotheses in this study are simply common sense hunches or guesses. For example, it seems a reasonable assumption that relationships defined as meaningful (question 6) will be rated more highly by respondents receiving the Meaningful Relationships Questionnaire than they rate questions 7 and 8. Moreover, it makes sense or seems reasonable that relationships that are m/s/f will be rated fairly highly on relational qualities (questions 9–12) and on relational themes and components (questions 13–22). Therefore, this study is more exploratory in nature than it is a formal hypothesis-testing research project.

What Makes Our Relationships Meaningful, Satisfying, or Fulfilling?

6. Respondents completing the Meaningful Relationships Questionnaire will rate the extent to which their meaningful relationships have significance, value, or importance (question 6) more highly than these relationships bring enjoyment, pleasure, or contentment (question 7), and more highly than they thrive or flourish (question 8). The same pattern will hold for respondents completing the other two questionnaires (responses to question 7 will be higher than for responses to questions 6 and 8 for respondents completing the Satisfying Relationships Questionnaire, and responses to question 8 will be higher than for questions 6 and 7 for respondents completing the Fulfilling Relationships Questionnaire).

7. Respondents will rate their responses to the four questions about m/s/f relationships qualities (questions 9, 10, 11, and 12) fairly highly (4.5 to 5.5), and their responses to the ten questions about m/s/f relationships themes (questions 13–22) also fairly highly (4.5 to 5.5). Similarly, respondents will rate most of the three descriptors for each quality and the three descriptors for each theme fairly highly (4.5 to 5.5).

Results

A summary of questionnaire results for each question is presented in appendix 12. Let's examine, then, whether or not the results confirm or disconfirm our hypotheses.

1. What fresh insights may we gain into the meanings of m/s/f?
    Several recurring themes, and several unique themes, are apparent and offer fresh insights as predicted. In particular, *mutuality* is a prominent theme for satisfying relationships respondents (cited 12 times) and secondary theme for both meaningful and fulfilling relationships respondents (cited 7 times each). *Caring, loving, and kind* is a secondary recurring theme for all three relationships respondents

What Makes Our Relationships Meaningful, Satisfying, or Fulfilling?

(cited 7 times each for meaningful and fulfilling relationships respondents and 4 times for satisfying relationships respondents). *Trust, respect, honesty, and authenticity/acceptance* is the most prominent theme for both meaningful (cited 17 times) and fulfilling (cited 16 times) relationships respondents yet is nearly missing for satisfying relationships respondents (only respect is cited 5 times). Likewise, *communication* is a theme for both meaningful (cited 7 times) and fulfilling (cited 3 times) relationships respondents, and not at all for satisfying relationships respondents. And then *enjoyment, fun, and laughter* is a secondary theme for both satisfying relationships (cited 5 times) and fulfilling relationships respondents (cited 3 times) and missing for meaningful relationships respondents. Finally, *acceptance* is the most prominent and a unique theme for satisfying relationships respondents (cited 16 times) and *comfortable* is a prominent and unique theme for fulfilling relationships respondents (cited 12 times).

2. How many m/s/f relationships do respondents have?

As predicted, nearly 80 percent of respondents have either 4–10 or 10–30 relationships (39 percent of our 80 total respondents for each). While this pattern holds true for satisfying relationships respondents (38 percent for each), a different pattern is apparent for meaningful relationships respondents (46 percent have 10–30 while 32 percent have 4–10) and for fulfilling relationship respondents (46 percent have 4–10 and 32 percent have 10–30).

The prediction that the number of respondents with meaningful relationships will be substantially higher (30–60 or higher) than for respondents with either satisfying or fulfilling relationships (4–10 or 10–30) is not confirmed. However, the prediction that few respondents will report having either very few relationships (3 or fewer) or very many relationships (100 or more) is confirmed. In fact, only 10 percent of respondents have 3 or fewer relationships and only 1 percent have 100 or more relationships.

What Makes Our Relationships Meaningful, Satisfying, or Fulfilling?

3. Among what type of personal relationships are most respondents' m/s/f relationships?

    The prediction here is confirmed for both meaningful and satisfying relationship respondents: most (over 60 percent) of their personal relationships are with family members and good friends. The same is true for fulfilling relationships respondents among family members (43 percent) but not for good friends (only 7 percent), although nearly half (46 percent) selected the "several of the above" option.[2]

4. In respondents relationships as a whole, to what extent are they m/s/f?

    Responses here are slightly lower than expected—slightly less than 5.0 rather than between 5 and 6.

5. How do respondents rate the overall health of their m/s/f relationships?

    Responses here are also slightly lower than expected—barely 5.0 rather than between 5 and 6.

6. To what extent do respondents' m/s/f relationships have significance, value, or importance?

    Responses here are similar among m/s/f relationships respondents, thereby not confirming expectations. Overall, responses are quite high for relationships having significance, value, or importance (5.7), fairly high for bringing enjoyment, pleasure, or contentment (5.4), and around 5.0 for thriving or flourishing. The only exception is for satisfying relationships respondents having a considerably lower thriving or flourishing response (4.3) than did meaningful respondents (5.4) or fulfilling respondents (4.9).

---

2. Also recall that these respondents could not select more than one answer, so their responses are likely skewed. For example, while they could not select more than one answer, 46 percent selected "several of the above"—a considerably higher percentage than for meaningful relationship respondents (32 percent) or satisfying relationship respondents (26 percent). Had they been able to select more than one answer, the impact on other response options is unclear.

What Makes Our Relationships Meaningful, Satisfying, or Fulfilling?

7. To what extent do respondents' m/s/f relationships bring enjoyment, pleasure, or contentment?

    See responses to question 6.

8. To what extent to respondents' m/s/f relationships thrive or flourish?

    See responses to question 6.

9. Do respondents rate their responses to the four questions about the qualities of m/s/f relationships (questions 9–12) fairly highly (4.5 to 5.5), and their responses to the ten questions about themes of m/s/f relationships (questions 13–22) also fairly highly (4.5 to 5.5)? And similarly, do respondents rate most of their three descriptors for each quality and their three descriptors for each theme fairly highly (4.5 to 5.5)?

    Respondent responses to questions 9–12 are confirmed: all are rated fairly highly—between 5.0 and 5.2.

    Similarly, respondent responses to the three relational quality descriptors are confirmed: all are rated fairly highly (4.5 to 5.4). Interestingly, responses to questions 9a (4.5), 9b (4.6), and 9c (4.7) are each considerably lower than for question 9 (5.0). And responses for questions 10a (5.4), 10b (5.4), and 10c (5.4) are each considerably higher than for question 10 (5.0).

    Respondent responses to questions 13–22 are also confirmed: all are rated fairly highly—between 4.5 (question 17) and 5.6 (question 15).

    Similarly, respondent responses to the three component descriptors for each theme are mostly confirmed: all are rated fairly highly (4.5 to 5.5) except one is rated slightly lower (4.3 for responses to question 22b, *participating in religious or spiritual rituals or practices*) and one is rated slightly higher (5.6 for responses to question 18c, *genuineness and integrity*).

    Interestingly, responses to questions 15a (4.8), 15b (5.0), and 15c (5.2) are each considerably lower than for question 15 (5.6). And responses to questions 17a (4.6), 17b (4.8), and 17c (5.4) are all higher than for question 17 (4.5).

What Makes Our Relationships Meaningful, Satisfying, or Fulfilling?

Three other results warrant comment. First, responses to question 14b, *respect and reciprocity*, are higher (5.4) than responses to questions 14 (4.9), 14a (5.0), and 14c (4.9). Second, responses to question 19c, *nurture and support one another*, are higher (5.4) than responses to questions 19 (5.1), 19a (4.8), and 19b (4.8). And third, responses to question 17c, *picking up right where you left off*, are higher (5.4) than responses to questions 17 (4.5), 17a (4.6), and 17b (4.8).

One final result of note: it is striking that there are only slight differences among m/s/f respondents in their answers to questions 9–22, including questions a, b, and c. Remarkably, there are only two exceptions. First, for question 12a, *gain insight into yourself*, for satisfying relationships respondents, responses are considerably lower (4.65) than responses for meaningful relationships respondents (5.1) and fulfilling relationships respondents (5.1). And second, for question 22b, *participating in religious or spiritual rituals or practices*, meaningful relationships respondent responses are considerably lower (3.9) than responses for satisfying relationship respondents (4.5) and fulfilling relationship respondents (4.5).

Observations and Discussion

1. Surprisingly, respondents in this study have two meanings in common when asked to define *meaningful, satisfying,* and *fulfilling*: *mutuality* (a prominent meaning for "satisfying" and secondary meanings for "meaningful" and "fulfilling") and *loving, caring, and kind* (a secondary meaning for all three words). It is perplexing that neither of these meanings is included in this study's composite definition for each word: *significance, value, and importance* for meaningful relationships; *enjoyment, pleasure, or contentment* for satisfying relationships; and *thrive or flourish* for fulfilling

What Makes Our Relationships Meaningful, Satisfying, or Fulfilling?

relationships. I expected respondents to define each word using dictionary-type descriptors. Instead, they define all three words in terms of qualities, likenesses, or behaviors. In reality, they *describe* their experience of each word rather than *define* the meaning of each word.

Perhaps they were thinking in terms of the initial research question: What makes your relationships meaningful, satisfying, or fulfilling? I asked for one or two (or more) brief responses from which ten themes and components of m/s/f relationships were derived and then tested in questions 13–22. More will be said about this observation later.

Besides "mutuality" and "loving, kind, and caring," the most prominent word cluster used to define "meaningful" and "fulfilling" is *trust, respect, honesty, and authenticity/acceptance*. And the most prominent word cluster used to define "satisfying" centers in *acceptance*, and includes such experiences as being known, openness, intimate, vulnerability, heard and seen, comfortable, empathy, safe, understanding, excited to see, and interest in being together. Likewise, a prominent word cluster used to define "fulfilling" centers in *comfortable*, and includes such descriptors as partnership, quality time, shared commitments, thankful, tending to one another, resonant, peaceful, intimacy, vulnerability, international and unconditional.[3] And then, *enjoyment, fun, and laughter* are secondary meanings for both "satisfying" and "fulfilling"—and the only overlap with this study's dictionary-type composite definitions (*enjoyment, pleasure, or contentment* for "satisfying" relationships).

Let's summarize the "fresh insights" we've gained thus far.

First, it is insightful to learn that there is one primary theme for meaningful relationships:

- Trust, respect, honesty, and authenticity

---

3. Note that "intimate" and "vulnerable" appear in both word clusters, and "comfortable" is included as an *acceptance* descriptor.

What Makes Our Relationships Meaningful, Satisfying, or Fulfilling?

And three secondary themes:

- Mutuality
- Caring, loving, and kind
- Communication

Second, we learn that there are two primary themes for satisfying relationships:

- Acceptance
- Mutuality

And two secondary themes:

- Enjoyable, fun, and laughter
- Caring, loving, and kind

And third, it is insightful to learn that there are two primary themes for fulfilling relationships:

- Trust, honesty, respect, and acceptance
- Comfortable

And four secondary themes:

- Mutuality
- Caring, loving, and kind
- Communication
- Enjoyment, fun, and laughter

It is also worth noting that words respondents use to define "meaningful," "satisfying," and "fulfilling" match or are similar to five of the ten themes and word cluster components of m/s/f relationships: mutuality, enjoyment, communication, being oneself/known (similar to acceptance), and presence (similar to comfortable). Connection, time, growth, work, and transcendence are missing. Likewise, and perhaps not surprisingly, there is overlap between three of the four relationship satisfaction qualities and behaviors: communication, being oneself (acceptance), and

What Makes Our Relationships Meaningful, Satisfying, or Fulfilling?

interpersonal security and warmth (comfortable). Only the quality and behavior of personal support and growth is missing.

2. While 80 percent of respondents have either 4–10 or 10–30 personal relationships, it is perplexing that whereas satisfying relationship respondents have an equal number of personal relationships (38 percent have 4–10 and 38 percent have 10–30), the distribution is unequal and reversed for meaningful relationship respondents (46 percent have 10–30 personal relationships and 32 percent have 4–10 personal relationships) and fulfilling relationship respondents (46 percent have 4–10 personal relationships and 32 percent have 10–30 personal relationships). Why might the distribution of personal relationships be evenly split between 4–10 and 10–30 for satisfying relationship respondents? And is there something about meaningful relationships that produces a greater number of personal relationships and something about fulfilling relationships that results in a lesser number of personal relationships? While these results may seem puzzling on the surface, they match my own experience in some respects. As mentioned in the conclusions of the earlier research project, I have considerably more meaningful personal relationships than either satisfying or fulfilling ones. Let's look a little more closely at the relational dynamics of this discrepancy.

As noted earlier, I have a meaningful relationship with all of my 191 family members, friends, good friends, and colleagues—they are significant, valuable, or important. We've spent quality time together, enjoyed each other's presence, had interest in one another's interests, respected and trusted each other, appreciated each other's uniqueness, and made a positive impact on each other's lives and worlds. With colleagues we've done important work together and made significant contributions from our efforts. But are these relationships also satisfying and fulfilling? Well, not necessarily. In fact, I don't expect that my relationships with all of them will become either satisfying or fulfilling. I do find that my *close personal relationships* with good friends and with some family members, friends, and colleagues are satisfying or fulfilling. Overall, I have 32 satisfying relationships—those that bring enjoyment, pleasure, or contentment. These are mostly among family members (12), good friends (11), and colleagues (8); only 1 is a friend. These are people who I see regularly and with whom I experience the relational qualities of openness, acceptance, warmth, and growth. Friends are nearly missing from these relationships because I don't see most of them in multiple settings or often enough to become satisfying. It is not that my friends are unimportant or insignificant (they are, remember, *meaningful* relationships). Rather, we just don't spend much time together or see each other often. For example, I have a meaningful relationship with all of my neighborhood friends, but not necessarily satisfying relationships with most of them. Our paths cross only occasionally and for brief periods of time. The same is true of most of my other friends, many of whom are former parishioners. And then overall, I have 49 fulfilling relationships—those that thrive or flourish. These are among family members (28), friends (11), and good friends (10) with whom I have ongoing close personal relationships and experience many of the ten relational themes of connection, mutuality, enjoyment, communication, time, being oneself/known, work, growth, presence, and transcendence. And even though I may not see some of these people often or regularly in person, our personal relationship continues to thrive or flourish. Colleagues are mostly missing from these relationships because while they are all meaningful and some satisfying, our close personal relationship did not continue after we stopped working together or develop into fulfilling relationships.[4]

---

4. It should be noted that there are a few family members and good friends that are also colleagues.

What Makes Our Relationships Meaningful, Satisfying, or Fulfilling?

Coincidentally only one other person has more than 100 personal relationships—one of my three brothers who has more than 200 fulfilling relationships. He defines "fulfilling" as "enjoy being with." When I asked him to define "meaningful" and "satisfying" and provide the number and types of these relationships, I learned that he makes no distinction among m/s/f. He simply has more than 200 meaningful, satisfying, and fulfilling relationships among a wide array of family members, friends, good friends, and colleagues—all of whom he considers close friends, particularly among members of his church community whom he enjoys being with and working together.

Whereas we've discovered that there are recurring and unique themes among respondent definitions of m/s/f, I wonder if in reality many are like my brother and make no distinction among m/s/f. Or perhaps they consider m/s/f as a composite—meaningful *and* satisfying *and* fulfilling. From the beginning of my research in graduate school fifty years ago and continuing throughout subsequent research projects, I've worded my research question to allow for distinction among them—what makes your relationships meaningful, satisfying, *or* fulfilling? Even though I've consistently used the distinctive "or" rather than the composite "and," I now wonder if both conjunctions result in respondents considering their m/s/f as a whole or in totality. Or perhaps some respondents make a distinction while others do not. In fact, when I asked respondents for one or two (or more) brief responses to my research question in the earlier research project, very few made a distinction between m/s/f in their replies.[5] In any event, in this follow-up research project respondents used their own descriptive definitions of what m/s/f relationships are like in their experience

---

5. And for respondents who do include all three (see the brief reflections in appendix 13), it is apparent that they understand "meaningful," "satisfying," and "fulfilling" very differently.

rather than using either the dictionary or composite definitions in their questionnaire responses.

3. As predicted, most respondent personal relationships are among family members and good friends—over 60 percent for both meaningful and satisfying relationship respondents. The pattern is true for fulfilling relationship respondents among family members, but not good friends. Unfortunately, fulfilling relationship respondents could not select more than one answer, and nearly half (46 percent) selected the option "several of the above." Had they been able to select more than one answer, I expect their responses would be similar to meaningful and satisfying relationships respondents—although there is no way to confirm this expectation.

4. It is puzzling why responses to respondents relationships as a whole being m/s/f, and also to the overall health of their m/s/f relationships, are slightly lower than expected—both at or slightly below 5.0 rather than between 5.0 and 6.0. Apparently, both respondent m/s/f relationships as a whole and the overall health of their m/s/f relationships are in the "fine" to "very fine" range (4.0–5.0) rather than in the "very fine" to "excellent" range (5.0–6.0). Neither is out the ordinary or even in an "average" range—just slightly lower than expected. It appears that I simply overestimated respondent responses. It is unclear why relationships as a whole responses are considerably lower for satisfying relationship respondents (4.4) than for meaningful (4.96) or fulfilling (4.89) ones. Apparently, relationships as a whole are more meaningful and fulfilling than satisfying.

5. Unlike predictions for responses to question 7 (m/s/f relationships have significance, value, or importance), question 8 (m/s/f relationships bring enjoyment, pleasure, or contentment), and question 9 (m/s/f relationships thrive or flourish), responses are fairly similar among m/s/f relationships on all three questions. Since respondents do not define

What Makes Our Relationships Meaningful, Satisfying, or Fulfilling?

m/s/f in these terms, these results are not surprising. Even so, responses for these three questions are relatively high (4.9 to 5.7), although it is unclear why there is considerable variance among them.

For example, while it is clear that most m/s/f respondents have very meaningful (5.7) and satisfying (5.4) relationships and quite fulfilling ones (4.9), it is unclear why their fulfilling relationship responses are considerably lower than their meaningful and satisfying relationship ones. In this instance, it appears that relationships are more meaningful and satisfying than fulfilling. Also, it is unclear why satisfying relationships respondents have considerably lower thriving or flourishing responses (4.3) than do meaningful respondents (5.4) or fulfilling respondents (4.9). In this instance, it appears that relationships are more meaningful and fulfilling than satisfying—even as we learned earlier that respondents' relationships as a whole are more meaningful and fulfilling than satisfying.

6. Responses to questions 9–12 are all rated fairly high (5.0–5.2), meaning that m/s/f relationship respondents are quite able to be open in their communication, be themselves, experience interpersonal security and warmth, and experience personal support and growth. Moreover, all three relational quality descriptors are also rated fairly high. Two results of interest warrant comment. First, the three ways respondents can be open in their communication have somewhat lower results (around 4.6) than their overall communication openness (around 5.0). Perhaps the negative bent to these descriptors (e.g., *open up and express your fears and doubts*, *tell others about your feelings*, and *share your personal problems*) play a role in this discrepancy.[6] And second, the three

---

6. These three descriptors were taken from the twelve-item interpersonal relationships satisfaction inventory. In the future, consideration should be given to include more positive descriptors or to reword them to be less problem-centered. For example, several descriptions in the forty-item IRSI might be considered, including: "Can you talk about your dreams and ambitions?"

What Makes Our Relationships Meaningful, Satisfying, or Fulfilling?

ways respondents can be themselves have somewhat higher results (around 5.4) than being themselves overall (around 5.0). Here, perhaps the positive nature of these descriptors (e.g., *respecting your ideas and opinions, being able to laugh at yourselves,* and *experiencing trust and empathy*) elevate the results of these three descriptors.[7]

7. Responses to questions 13–22 are also rated fairly highly (4.5–5.6), meaning that respondents in their m/s/f relationships are quite able to connect, have mutual interests, enjoy being together, communicate well, spend time together, feel free to be themselves, learn and grow, work at their relationships, be present and available, and feed their souls and spirits. Likewise, responses to the three component descriptors for each theme are nearly all rated fairly highly (4.5 to 5.5). Three results warrant further comment.

First, results for the three ways respondents enjoy being together are somewhat lower (around 5.0) than their overall enjoyment (5.6). Two components seem to have put some respondents off stride (*camaraderie and a spirit of adventure* and *lightheartedness and fun-loving*). Perhaps they feel these two components are overly "playful" or hedonistic and thereby less attractive activities.[8] And then results for the three ways respondents spend time together are all higher (4.6–5.4) than for spending time together overall (4.5). Respondents seem to respond particularly positively to the component *picking up right where you left off after an absence* (5.4). The other two components, *taking initiative to be together* (4.6) and *at ease with silence* (4.8), are similar to the overall result for spending time together (4.5) and may reveal a quandary for respondents: some personal

---

(see item 9 in appendix 3), "Do you have someone to go to in any situation?" (see item 14 in appendix 3), and "Can you talk about those things in your lives which most matter?" (see item 27 in appendix 3).

7. In any event, these three descriptors are a good fit for "being yourself."

8. Nonetheless, they appear to be sufficiently appealing activities to most respondents.

What Makes Our Relationships Meaningful, Satisfying, or Fulfilling?

relationships are highly valued even though the partners may not spend time together in person frequently—as evident by their capacity to pick up right where they left off after an absence.[9]

Second, two other results are particularly interesting. Results for one component of having mutual interests, *respect and reciprocity* (5.4), is somewhat higher than responses to overall mutual interest (4.9) and the other two components—*common beliefs and values* (5.0) and *shared understanding and experience* (4.9). Apparently respect and reciprocity is simply a more highly valued component than overall mutuality and the other two components. Next, results for one component of learning and growing, *nurture and support one another* (5.4), are somewhat higher than for overall learning and growing (5.1) and the other two components—*openness to change* (4.8) and *welcome challenges and differences* (4.8). It appears, then, that nurture and support is viewed more positively than openness to change and welcoming challenges.[10]

Third, we have the striking observation that there are only slight differences among m/s/f respondents in their answers to questions 9–22, including questions a, b, and c. These results verify the usefulness of these ten themes and components as measures of m/s/f relationships. In fact, there are only two exceptions. First, results for *gaining insight into yourself* as a way to experience personal support and growth are considerably lower for satisfying relationships respondents (4.65) than results for meaningful relationships respondents (5.1) and fulfilling relationships respondents (5.1). Apparently, several satisfying relationships respondents are both growing and learning and feel

---

9. This quandary is inherent in the variety of ways people spend time together, including individual preferences (e.g., in person, online, phone calls, texting, etc.). Perhaps adding a qualifier such as spending "quality" time together would be helpful for some respondents.

10. These two results do not appear to have significantly affected overall respondent responses.

supported, but simply not gaining much insight into themselves. In this instance it seems that two or three respondents reported lower responses than most people, thereby bringing down overall group results. And second, results for *participating in religious or spiritual rituals or practices* as a component of feeding your souls and spirit is considerably lower (3.9) for meaningful relationship respondents than for satisfying relationships respondents (4.5) and fulfilling relationship respondents (4.5). There appears to be nothing of substance to explain this disparity among respondents. Again, this disparity appears to be a statistical anomaly. Seven out of eleven respondents who rated this component very low (with a "1" or "2" on the "not well" end of the six-point scale) got randomly selected to receive the meaningful relationships questionnaire. Only one was a satisfying relationships respondent and three were fulfilling relationships respondents.

Conclusions

1. For respondents in this study, the definitions, themes, and word clusters for "meaningful," "satisfying," and "fulfilling" relationships have more in common than they are distinct. *Mutuality* is a common word and *loving, kind, and caring* a common theme for all three relationships. *Trust, respect, honesty, and authenticity/acceptance* is a theme and *communication* a word used to define both "meaningful" and "fulfilling" relationships. *Enjoyable, fun, and laughter* are themes shared by "satisfying" and "fulfilling" relationships. Only *acceptance* is a distinctive word cluster for "satisfying" relationships, and *comfortable* a distinctive word cluster for "fulfilling" relationships.

2. There is very little correlation between or overlap among the descriptive-type "definitions" respondents use in this study

What Makes Our Relationships Meaningful, Satisfying, or Fulfilling?

for "meaningful," "satisfying," or "fulfilling" relationships and the typical dictionary-type definitions, including the distinctive composite definitions used in questions 6, 7, and 8. In other words, respondents in this study seem to consider their meaningful, satisfying, and fulfilling relationships as a whole or composite rather than make a distinction between them. They appear to be used more interchangeably than with nuanced distinctions.[11] The similarity in response results among respondents receiving the three distinct questionnaires is therefore not surprising. Furthermore, the interpretation of results must account for this likelihood.

3. Most personal relationships for all respondents are among their family members and good friends.

4. Relationships as a whole are very meaningful for meaningful relationship respondents, fulfilling for fulfilling relationship respondents, and quite satisfying for satisfying relationship respondents. Clearly, though, relationships are more meaningful and fulfilling than satisfying.

5. The overall health of relationships for all respondents is relatively high, though slightly lower than expected.

6. Most respondents have very meaningful and satisfying relationships, and quite fulfilling relationships. While meaningful and satisfying responses are higher overall than fulfilling ones, satisfying relationships respondents have considerably lower fulfilling relationships responses than meaningful or fulfilling relationships respondents. While mixed, evidence is growing that relationships are more meaningful and fulfilling than satisfying.

7. In their relationships, respondents are quite able to be open in their communication; be themselves; experience interpersonal security and warmth; and experience personal support and growth. They also do quite well on the three descriptors for each of the four relational qualities.

---

11. Even AI assistance from ChatGPT generates overlapping definitions and blurred distinctions.

What Makes Our Relationships Meaningful, Satisfying, or Fulfilling?

8. In their relationships, respondents are quite able to connect; have mutual interests; enjoy being together; communicate well; spend time together; feel free to be themselves; learn and grow; work at their relationships; be present and available; and feed their souls and spirits. They also do quite well on the three component descriptors for each of the ten themes.

SUMMARY

In chapter 2, we noted that the four qualities that surface in the 1975 research (communication openness, being oneself, interpersonal security and warmth, and personal support and growth) are in accord with no particular then-current theory of relationship satisfaction. Moreover, a new eclectic theory is likely to evolve from the findings of this study and future research. So, let's summarize where we are in identifying such a theory of meaningful, satisfying, or fulfilling personal relationships.

While the original research focuses on interpersonal relationship satisfaction, our review of updated and current social science literature in chapter 1 also includes the other two original constructs: meaningful relationships and fulfilling relationships. And we now have three eclectic, composite definitions: *meaningful* relationships have significance, value, or importance; *satisfying* relationships bring enjoyment, pleasure, or contentment; and *fulfilling* relationships thrive or flourish.

We also now confirm that there are four predictors or determinates of m/s/f personal relationships: *openness, acceptance, warmth,* and *growth*. And we can expand our understanding of what makes our personal relationships m/s/f to include *connection, mutuality, enjoyment, communication, time, being oneself/ known, growth, work, presence,* and *transcendence*.

We also now have operational definitions for these four qualities and ten themes.

Openness means sharing, risking, and assertiveness. It also means having someone to go to in any situation, talking about

What Makes Our Relationships Meaningful, Satisfying, or Fulfilling?

those things in life which most matter, and talking about our dreams and ambitions. *Acceptance* means listening, trusting, and empathy. Also respecting one another's ideas and opinions, being able to laugh at ourselves, and experiencing trust and empathy with one another. *Growth* means supporting, empowering, and curiosity. Also gaining insight into ourselves, feeling like we're growing and learning, and feeling supported by one another. And *warmth* means caring, connecting, and mutuality. Also feeling that we are valued and wanted, feeling affection and care for one another, and feeling important to and safe with one another.

Connection means belonging and togetherness, having chemistry and "clicking" with one another, and giving attention to and expressing appreciation for one another. *Mutuality* means having common beliefs and values, respect and reciprocity, and shared understanding and experiences. *Enjoyment* means camaraderie and a spirit of adventure, lightheartedness and fun-loving, and bonds of warmth and affection. *Communication* means free-flowing and ease of conversation, listening and being understood, and honesty and authenticity. *Time* means taking initiative to be together, being at ease with silence, and picking up right where we left off after an absence. *Being ourselves* means marked by acceptance and affirmation, vulnerability and safety, and genuineness and integrity. *Growth* means openness to change, welcoming challenges and differences, and nurturing and supporting one another. *Work* means facing and overcoming obstacles in our relationships, setting and keeping boundaries, and letting go and practicing forgiveness as appropriate. *Presence* means showing up and being attentive, feeling comfortable with one another, and feeling valued and respected. And *transcendence* means connecting to something greater than ourselves, participating in religious or spiritual rituals or practices, and creating a sense of community or soul friendships.

Besides four qualities and ten themes of m/s/f personal relationships, we can operationalize *relationship satisfaction* in close personal relationships to mean willingness to invest and engage; emotional closeness and affection; trust and acceptance; care and support; similar and mutual interests; feeling safe and comfortable;

What Makes Our Relationships Meaningful, Satisfying, or Fulfilling?

talking through and working out arguments and conflicts; and being open and feeling understood in our communication.

And we now have Four C's of relational health and satisfaction in organizational relationships, including *community*, *communication*, *character*, and *collaboration*, along with six ways each is operationalized (see appendix 5). Moreover, there is a fit between ways the Four C's are demonstrated and the themes and components of communication, connection, and growth.

In short, we now have a theory of meaningful, satisfying, or fulfilling relationships that includes eclectic or composite definitions for each construct, along with four research-based qualities and ten research-based themes of m/s/f personal relationships, and the Four C's signs of relational health in organizational relationships—all with operational definitions. We also have three corresponding measurement instruments: our original Interpersonal Relationship Satisfaction Inventories (see appendices 2 and 3, and note: both measure m/s/f relationships, not just relationship satisfaction); a new Meaningful, Satisfying, or Fulfilling Relationships Inventory (see appendix 9); and a new Relationship Satisfaction Inventory (see appendix 14).

PRACTICAL APPLICATIONS

1. What one or two words or phrases best define a meaningful relationship for you? How about a satisfying one? And how about a fulfilling one?

2. How many meaningful relationships do you have? How many satisfying ones? How many fulfilling ones? What do you learn about yourself and your relationships from comparing and contrasting your responses? For example, note of which relationships you have the most and the least. How many people are on multiple lists? For example, how many of your personal relationships are both meaningful and satisfying, meaningful and fulfilling, satisfying and fulfilling, and all three?

What Makes Our Relationships Meaningful, Satisfying, or Fulfilling?

3. Among what types of relationships are your meaningful relationships (family members, friends, good friends, and colleagues)? How about for your satisfying ones? And for your fulfilling ones? What do you learn about yourself and your relationships from your responses?

4. In your meaningful, satisfying, or fulfilling relationships, to what extent do they have significance, value, or importance to you?[12] To what extent do they bring you enjoyment, pleasure, or contentment? And to what extent do they thrive or flourish? What do you learn about yourself and your relationships from your responses?

5. Assess the quality of your meaningful, satisfying, or fulfilling relationships using questions 9, 10, 11, and 12 in appendix 11. What do you learn about yourself and your relationships from your responses?

6. In your meaningful, satisfying, or fulfilling relationships, use questions 13–22 in appendix 11 to assess the extent to which you connect with one another; have mutual interests; enjoy being with one another; communicate well with one another; spend time together; are free to be yourselves; learn and grow; work at your relationships; are present and available to one another; and feed your souls and spirits. What do you learn about yourself and your relationships from your responses?

---

12. For this and related questions, use a scale of 1 to 6 where 1 equals never or very little and 6 equals always or very much.

4

Making Relationships Meaningful, Satisfying, or Fulfilling

IN CHAPTER 1 WE learn that meaningful relationships are ones that have significance, purpose, and coherence. Also, character strengths can cultivate meaningful relationships. Next, we discover that fulfilling relationships are ones that bring wellbeing and flourishing and include positive emotion, engagement, meaning, positive relationships, and accomplishment. Wellbeing and flourishing can also be created by character strengths and are closely linked to meaningful and satisfying relationships. And then we find that satisfying relationships are ones with a broad array of features including closeness and support, trust and acceptance, balance and similarities, safety and caring, comfort and security, investment and affection, and communication and conflict management.

In chapter 2 we learn that four qualities make our relationships meaningful, satisfying, or fulfilling: communication openness; being oneself; interpersonal security and warmth; and personal support and growth. There are also twelve guidelines for these four qualities. And then we discover ten themes that describe what makes our relationships meaningful, satisfying, or fulfilling:

Making Relationships Meaningful, Satisfying, or Fulfilling

connection, mutuality, enjoyment, communication, time, being oneself, growth, work, presence, and transcendence. Moreover, we find a fit between the Four C's of relational health and satisfaction (community, communication, character, and collaboration) and the themes of communication, connection, and growth.

And in chapter 3 we learn that people have 4–10 or 10–30 relationships mainly among their family members and good friends. Also, their relationships as a whole are meaningful, satisfying, and fulfilling, and quite healthy overall. They have significance, value, and importance; they bring enjoyment, pleasure, or contentment; and they thrive and flourish. And in their meaningful, satisfying, and fulfilling relationships, they do well on the four qualities and ten themes.

But how do people go about making their relationships meaningful, satisfying, or fulfilling? Let's look more closely at the ways each of the four qualities and ten themes are expressed or experienced.

FOUR QUALITIES

It's Thursday night, time for a bimonthly Conversations on the Way sharing and support group Zoom meeting to begin. Normal chitchat takes place as people join the meeting. Then the facilitator poses the evening's sharing questions drawn from the group's reading assignment of *We Will Be Jaguars: A Memoir of My People* by Nemonte Nenquimo: "If people were to visit us from Mars, what are one or two things you think they'd first notice?" Also, "If you heard they were around, what are one or two things you would be curious about?"

After twenty or thirty minutes of sharing, including catching up on one another's lives, the group moves into their discussion of the evening's reading assignment. During their time together, group members feel free to speak up and share what's on their hearts and minds. Everyone's ideas are important and members value each other's personal knowledge and experience. Members try to maintain an open mind, listening objectively and without

What Makes Our Relationships Meaningful, Satisfying, or Fulfilling?

judgment. Disagreements are expressed freely and in a friendly manner, keeping in mind that other people's views make sense to them. Clear communication is practiced, including listening to understand one another, asking for clarification of unclear points, and perception-checking if communication begins to break down. Members help each other participate, letting one another talk, showing interest in what each other has to say, inviting one another to speak, and making sure everyone has opportunity to share. Sometimes smiles do more to further discussion than best arguments. Members also help one another learn and support each other's personal growth. An atmosphere of warmth and affection and a culture of care have developed over the years. Indeed, their conversation is a pleasant and enjoyable experience for all. Since these group members have a common faith orientation, they conclude their time together with prayer requests and a closing prayer.

This sharing and support group scenario demonstrates four qualities that make their relationships meaningful, satisfying, and fulfilling: openness, acceptance, warmth, and growth. Drawing on insights gained from previous chapters, here are ways group members experience these four qualities.

1. Communication Openness

Ways we can be open in our communication

- Sharing about our dreams and ambitions
- Having someone to go to in any situation
- Sharing about things in life that matter most
- Risking and being vulnerable
- Being assertive and genuine

Making Relationships Meaningful, Satisfying, or Fulfilling

2. Being Oneself

Ways we can be ourselves

- Listening to and respecting one another's ideas and opinions
- Being able to laugh at ourselves
- Experiencing trust and empathy

3. Interpersonal Security and Warmth

Ways we can experience interpersonal security and warmth

- Feeling that we are valued and wanted
- Feeling affection and caring for one another
- Feeling important to and safe with one another
- Connecting and having mutual interests

4. Personal Support and Growth

Ways we can experience personal support and growth

- Gaining insight into ourselves
- Feeling like we are growing and learning
- Feeling supported by one another
- Empowering one another
- Exercising curiosity

What Makes Our Relationships Meaningful, Satisfying, or Fulfilling?

TEN THEMES

The most important thing I do in my life is meet twice a month with colleagues in a clergy support group.[1] These colleagues are among my most rich and rewarding relationships. We meet once a month for a two-hour Zoom book discussion[2] and once a month as a four-hour in-person sharing and support group. Our purpose is to enable one another to experience personal and professional growth through trustful interaction with colleagues. We are present to, comfortable with, and value one another. We are interested in and invested in one another. There's mutual affection, appreciation, and respect. There is also a closeness and spirit of camaraderie and enjoyment among us. We allow time to express our deepest thoughts and feelings about needs and concerns that currently matter most in our lives. We feel heard, accepted, and affirmed by caring peers. Confidentiality is observed with freedom to share without fear of being judged or rejected. We practice active listening, offering appropriate feedback and clarifying questions. Accountability for specific change and growth is encouraged and supported. We conclude with a circle of prayer, and often with a lovingkindness meditation.[3]

As you can see, many of the ten themes of meaningful, satisfying, and fulfilling relationships are present in our life together. What, though, are practical ways to make our relationships meaningful, satisfying, or fulfilling? In the remainder of this chapter, for each of the ten themes, you'll first find brief quotations of distilled wisdom from research participants—family members, friends,

---

1. Members include a United Methodist minister, four Presbyterian (USA) ministers, and a UCC minister.

2. Among the books we've read and discussed are *The Powers That Be* by Walter Wink, *Braiding Sweetgrass* by Robin Wall Kimmerer, *Dear White Christians* by Jennifer Harvey, *How to Know a Person* by David Brooks, *Caste* by Isabel Wilkerson, *Postcolonial Imagination and Feminist Theology* by Kwok Pui-lan, *James* by Percival Everett, *America's Unholy Ghosts* by Joel Edward Goza, and *Good Energy* by Casey Means and Calley Means.

3. One member's own version has evolved, as follows: "May I be at peace. May my heart always be open. May I continue to awaken to divine light deep within and all around. May I be healed in all the ways I can be healed. May I be a source of healing for others extending out to all creation. In the name of Jesus."

good friends, and colleagues. And then look for an outline of practical wisdom drawn from previous chapters followed by "vignettes" that capture facets of the real-life experiences of research participants. A summary at the end features a "big picture" or "integrating" vignette along with conclusions.

1. Connection

Even though we move across the country we can stay connected through shared stories and experiences.

Some like-mindedness is needed, even if it is simply connecting as being human.

We can be together in silence comfortably.

We move through the world differently as a result of connecting to different experiences from our own.

Ways we connect with one another

- Developing closeness, belonging, and togetherness
- Having chemistry and "clicking" with one another
- Giving attention to and expressing appreciation for one another
- Finding common ground

Ways we share with one another

- Building relationships
- Affirming and supporting
- Bridging cultures

What Makes Our Relationships Meaningful, Satisfying, or Fulfilling?

Ways we treat one another

- Practicing humility
- Feeling compassion
- Showing kindness
- Demonstrating love

Vignettes

> It is important for me to have a give-and-take in conversations, whether I agree or not with the other's opinions. Sometimes you just feel connected to that other person from the first conversation, and I try to build on that connection to further the relationship in a meaningful way.[4]

* * *

> It seems like we have different kinds of relationships. We have close family ties, and these are built-in relationships, made more meaningful with connecting with one another. Many are some distance away, but visiting as much as possible keeps the bonds. Then we have friends who live nearby, probably mostly from churches. Again, connecting with one another through discussions, prayer, worship, sharing joys and concerns, eating together, doing activities together, even meetings are some of the ways we stay close to each other and keep our relationships meaningful.[5]

* * *

---

4. Email message to author, September 24, 2025. Note: I am grateful to the research participants for their permission to quote excerpts from their responses. To maintain confidentiality, their names will be largely omitted throughout.

5. Email message to author, September 24, 2025.

Making Relationships Meaningful, Satisfying, or Fulfilling

Children and family relationships center around unconditional love. At times, these relationships may not be satisfying when we experience cutoff or aberrant behaviors. Candor, commitment, and staying connected build trust to make those relationships deeply meaningful and fulfilling.[6]

2. Mutuality

There's a mutual give-and-take where no one person dominates.

Mutual compatibility or complementarity leads to "clicking" with each other.

I like people who are nice to me and like the same things— people who very kind and have similar interests.

Mutual trust, or faith in each other, gives a relationship a solid foundation.

Ways we have mutual interests

- Having common beliefs and values
- Respecting our differences and similarities
- Having shared understanding and experiences

Vignettes

My most meaningful relationships have a mutuality about them—I extend support and care and trust the others to support and care for me too. That involves vulnerability on both sides. Relationships are also satisfying

---

6. Email message to author, September 24, 2025.

What Makes Our Relationships Meaningful, Satisfying, or Fulfilling?

for me when they encompass the whole of life, e.g., I'm able to cry and share sad things as well as laugh and play, and I even enjoy the presence of another in the ordinary tasks of the day.[7]

* * *

Relationships are positive when they are reciprocal, mutual, and have the option to be vulnerable from time to time. For me, "reciprocal" means both parties initiate contact. "Mutual" means an even connection, not one where one person usually complains and the other listens or tries to solve, or one person feels "above" the other who is benefiting from their wisdom. "Vulnerable" means both can be honest without fear of judgment.[8]

* * *

What makes your relationships meaningful, satisfying, or fulfilling? Is there a commonality with another person? I can talk for hours with someone who wants to know more about Native American culture or has something that fulfills my interests in culture, Christianity, or music. That is an essence of a satisfying relationship for me.

I serve on the board of directors for a conference center and my first face-to-face meeting was rewarding in so many ways. I was asked by a couple to take some time after dinner to sit and visit with them about Native American culture. One of them had served the board for many years.

They shared with me their experiences of living in the American Southwest, exploring Native American culture, and also their time among tribal people in South Dakota. They gifted me with a "medicine bag" the next day, and I knew I had found new friends, and a "meaningful, satisfying, and fulfilling" relationship, in such a short time.[9]

---

7. Email message to author, September 24, 2025.
8. Email message to author, September 24, 2025.
9. I am grateful to Rev. Irvin Porter for his permission to include this response; email message to author, October 13, 2025.

Making Relationships Meaningful, Satisfying, or Fulfilling

* * *

As I age, I cherish more and more relationships that are nurturing. I don't have the emotional energy to deal with relationships that require constant giving to the exclusion of receiving.[10]

3. Enjoyment

We surprise one another and bring novelty to our relationship.

Anticipating and sharing time together make me feel better.

We have a shared sense of humor and make an effort to keep the relationship alive and vibrant.

Enjoying common interests and adventures is essential.

Ways we enjoy one another

- Experiencing camaraderie, zest, and a spirit of adventure
- Being lighthearted, good-humored, and fun-loving
- Having bonds of warmth and affection
- Experiencing happiness, pleasure, and contentment
- Being thankful and grateful
- Being joyful, hopeful, and positive

Vignettes

The things that make relationships meaningful to me are being able to talk to someone about whatever and getting

---

10. Email message to author, September 29, 2025.

What Makes Our Relationships Meaningful, Satisfying, or Fulfilling?

a new way to look at things. Also whether or not I can enjoy my time talking to someone, whether that's having fun or just feeling comfortable.[11]

* * *

Neighbors, including those we meet in church, lead to long-lasting relationships because of daily interaction, service projects, and working together. One unlikely relationship is a neighbor who has no faith and supports the other political party, yet because we share a sense of humor, a relationship is satisfying nonetheless.[12]

4. Communication

We are able to discuss important and complicated issues without coming unglued.

We are candid without being manipulative.

We go beyond small talk to share deeply about such matters of the heart as our joys, struggles, and concerns.

Quality communication includes give-and-take, listening, and responding appropriately.

Ways we communicate with one another

- Free-flowing and ease of conversation
- Listening and being understood
- Being honest and authentic
- Being technologically savvy

11. Email message to author, September 24, 2025.
12. Email message to author, September 24, 2025.

Making Relationships Meaningful, Satisfying, or Fulfilling

Vignettes

Meaningful conversations fill a practical, theoretical, and intellectual need, and I especially find "deep" exchanges as avenues to better understand others as well as appreciate them more. Such conversations are also what I recall the most when I think of individuals and how I "frame" my memories of them.[13]

* * *

What makes my relationships meaningful is that we are good listeners of one another. It reinforces the care and compassion that are necessary for a satisfying relationship. This doesn't mean that we always agree on everything, but we are willing to hear what each other is saying, compromise where possible, and accept differences so that we can always grow in the relationship. My closest relationships are ones where we give to each other without giving a second thought, don't expect anything in return, and there is always compassion. Love trumps all.[14]

* * *

Relationships become rich for me when both parties share from deep within themselves and see each other as equals. The interaction is satisfying when it includes equal parts of listening and sharing on both sides. Challenge and support are important elements of these relationships, as well as genuine acceptance.[15]

5. Time

We're able to pick up where we left off after an absence.

---

13. Email message to author, September 24, 2025.
14. Email message to author, September 24, 2025.
15. Email message to author, September 25, 2025.

What Makes Our Relationships Meaningful, Satisfying, or Fulfilling?

We respect one another's time and are present when we're together.

We build deep and valued relationships over time and without feeling rushed.

We prioritize quality time even when distance divides us.

Ways we spend time together

- Taking initiative to be together
- Being interested and invested
- Being at ease with silence

Vignettes

What makes my relationships meaningful, satisfying, or fulfilling? My answer is as simple as one word: "Time."[16]

* * *

I think relationships are meaningful when we can talk deeply about things or talk about many different kinds of topics. Also, it's important to me to have plenty of time with my really good friends. Time spent doing conversation, or time just working next to each other. I don't like it when someone negates me; I appreciate it when someone listens and is affirming. Not always agreement, that would be boring. I also like it when we can be sympathetic with each other.[17]

* * *

16. Email message to author, September 24, 2025.
17. Email message to author, September 24, 2025.

Making Relationships Meaningful, Satisfying, or Fulfilling

> I really appreciate the gift of time—that someone wants to spend time with me. I really appreciate being my authentic self and being forgiven when necessary. I feel fulfillment when I am fully seen and heard. I like to feel like I am adding something to the lives of those around me.[18]

6. Being Oneself/Known

Meaningful relationships make us feel heard and seen.

We are safe in our relationship to confide, grow, challenge occasionally, and celebrate.

We don't have to edit ourselves, knowing that we are accepted and loved just as we are.

I don't like to be "crowded," so respect for space in both a physical and emotional sense is important.

Ways we are free to be ourselves

- Being accepted, appreciated, affirmed, and loved
- Feeling safe to be vulnerable
- Being genuine and having integrity
- Having significance, value, and importance

Vignettes

> Honesty and vulnerability feel like key components to relationships that I particularly value. We share real life ups and downs, struggles and joys. I also feel valued

---

18. Email message to author, September 24, 2025.

in relationships where others do and say things that indicate they know me, actually know me. Therefore, a mutual commitment to know one another and sacrifice for one another brings deep meaning and fulfillment in relationships for me.[19]

* * *

Some of the most important things to me in my meaningful and fulfilling relationships are the ability to be vulnerable (emotional trust), to be open-minded without judgment, and to be supportive even if we disagree. Of course, working on a goal together creates a different level of meaning and fulfillment. Some attributes I find frequently in those I hold closest are compassion, understanding, patience, emotional intelligence, love, kindness, being service-oriented, and being collaborative.[20]

* * *

I find the most meaningful relationships to be ones where I feel I can be my authentic and truest self around someone. It lets my guard down, and that's when special moments come about. This means that they must show up without judgment, and I would do the same. It creates a safe space for us both to exist.[21]

7. Growth

We help each other become better people through being vulnerable, accountable, and deeply known.

Meaningful relationships change our perspective and facilitate growth.

We are challenged to explore a subject or trait outside our

---

19. Email message to author, October 23, 2025.
20. Email message to author, September 24, 2025.
21. Email message to author, October 17, 2025.

Making Relationships Meaningful, Satisfying, or Fulfilling

comfort zone with assurances that the possibility of failure doesn't really exist.

Meaningful relationships change us and affirm one another in healthy ways.

Ways we learn and grow

- Being open to change
- Welcoming challenges and differences
- Nurturing and supporting one another
- Offering wisdom and perspective
- Using our social intelligence
- Gaining a sense of purpose and direction
- Helping one another achieve our goals
- Thriving and flourishing

Ways we collaborate with one another

- Visioning and planning
- Discerning and decision-making
- Engaging one another's gifts
- Using power appropriately
- Partnering

Vignettes

When all is said and done, relationships can be positive, helpful, and growing, or they can be negative, degrading,

What Makes Our Relationships Meaningful, Satisfying, or Fulfilling?

and a weakening influence on an individual. I choose the first and would like to think that I avoid the latter.[22]

* * *

Shared interests help promote connection and fun activities, and differences promote growth and learning, as we hear and experience what is important to the other and why.[23]

* * *

"Brave space" includes and exceeds the concept of "safe place." Safety is not the end goal, but safety is necessary for trust and honesty to flourish. But brave space also involves risks—trying out new practices or even versions of ourselves. It includes the accountability and forgiveness required when hurt is caused or someone's boundaries are crossed or violated. It takes courage to care enough to challenge each other and to allow others to possibly grow away from us.[24]

8. *Work*

Relationships require a great deal of work—investments of time often not reciprocated.

Sometimes we need to work things out on our own.

We use our differences to find options that work for our partnership.

We have overcome difficult problems through listening to one another with respect for each other's point of view.

---

22. Email message to author, September 24, 2025.
23. Email message to author, September 25, 2025.
24. Email message to author, October 2, 2025.

Making Relationships Meaningful, Satisfying, or Fulfilling

Ways we work at our relationships

- Facing and overcoming obstacles
- Setting and keeping boundaries
- Being responsible
- Engaging conflict
- Letting go and practicing forgiveness as appropriate

Vignettes

> What's meaningful to me is having a partner and relationship that listens and helps me work through the hard times, and plan for the good times. I enjoy the fact that my partner views life and the world from a different perspective. That diversity helps when working through issues with life. We don't always start out on the same page but I am grateful that we work on issues as a team. "Let every person be quick to hear, slow to speak, slow to anger."[25]

* * *

> *The Road Back to You* by Ian Morgan Cron and Suzanne Stabile has been helpful in understanding my desires and motivations. My life's path has more clarity. *The 5 Love Languages* by Gary Chapman has also been formative in what I find meaningful, satisfying, or fulfilling in my relationships. Recently, I've found Don Miguel's work, *The Four Agreements*, *The Fifth Agreement*, and *The Mastery of Love* to be most significant for where I'm at in my journey. I've been more successful taking action in my life lately. I'm actively creating a new dream for my future, but with more awareness of what I value and desire this time. Forgiveness for the ones that have damaged me, and truly letting go, are my daily challenges.[26]

---

25. Email message to author, September 24, 2025.
26. Email message to author, October 4, 2025.

What Makes Our Relationships Meaningful, Satisfying, or Fulfilling?

9. Presence

We have someone who cares about your often boring day and is simply there to talk to you.

We are there for one another, especially through rough times.

We respect one other's time and are engaged when we're together.

We are engaged with one another in the moment rather than what's happening on our phones.

Ways we are present and available

- Showing up and being attentive
- Feeling comfortable with one another
- Feeling valued and respected

Vignettes

> A meaningful and satisfying relationship is one where the other person knows me and I know them (faults and all) and they are still my friend. One of my closest friends was Catholic and I am Protestant and we voted for different political parties. However, when my mother died unexpectedly, she stayed up all night with my sister and me while we wept and reminisced. In my friend's last days of life in a nursing home, I sat by her bed while she slept and visited with her when she was awake.[27]

* * *

---

27. Email message to author, September 24, 2025.

Making Relationships Meaningful, Satisfying, or Fulfilling

Through this battle with cancer I have discovered what true friendship is. My PEO sisters, the minute they heard about my cancer, stepped forward and have been taking me to all my chemo treatments and sitting with me through them. I didn't ask; they volunteered. The twelve chemo treatments were covered immediately, and several were waiting in the wings to fill in. I have tended to be on the giving end of relationships and not usually in need of help. This experience has helped me know true friendship.[28]

* * *

One of the most important aspects of meaningful, satisfying, and fulfilling relationships is intentionality—mutually giving attention to the other, initiating and spending time with each other, focusing on each other, being present and listening![29]

10. Transcendence

We live with awe and wonder, not getting so wrapped up in everyday stresses that we fail to appreciate and be thankful for the good things in our relationships.

We draw on immanent divinity or the presence of Spirit to develop our own path to personal health and wellbeing.

We build our relationships on love—it checks all the boxes of meaningful, satisfying, and fulfilling relationships.

We have deep gratitude and love of life, and fearless confidence in the universal beauty of our death transition.

---

28. Email message to author, September 27, 2025.
29. Email message to author, November 5, 2025.

What Makes Our Relationships Meaningful, Satisfying, or Fulfilling?

Ways we feed our souls and spirits

- Connecting to something greater than ourselves
- Doing justice and promoting peace
- Participating in religious or spiritual rituals or practices
- Creating a sense of community or soul friendships

Vignettes

> My relationships are made meaningful, satisfying, or fulfilling through the collaborative pursuit of truth and revelation as God's creation. Through experiencing together the communion of ourselves and God through art, nature, and family. Through weathering the highs and lows of life together as community.[30]

* * *

> I'd say that for a relationship to be meaningful it needs to feed my soul in some way. That in turn requires me to identify those qualities that I find nurturing; these include empathy with who I am as a person, humor, kindness, and ideally at least some level of spiritual and ideological compatibility. I know that a satisfying relationship is contingent on reciprocity and that I in turn need to provide something meaningful to this other individual.[31]

* * *

> *Anam Cara*, the Celtic words for "soul friend," is a friend who walks alongside. A deep, abiding friendship is formed. I have been blessed with several soul friends along the way in different seasons of my life.[32]

30. Email message to author, September 24, 2025.
31. Email message to author, September 24, 2025.
32. Email message to author, September 24, 2025.

Making Relationships Meaningful, Satisfying, or Fulfilling

SUMMARY

Here is an especially poignant, all-encompassing response to what makes our relationships meaningful, satisfying, or fulfilling. You'll find all four qualities and ten themes embedded or integrated. In short, it is an apt summary of what we have learned about relationships.

> When I think about the relationships I have that are the most meaningful to me, and have lasted over time, three elements come to mind: *attraction, engagement, intentionality.*
>
> I have many relationships that began with *acquaintance.* Something brought us together. Perhaps it was a chance meeting, an introduction by a friend, or a necessity that one of us had which led to our meeting.
>
> However, among these, those relationships that went further were motivated by an *attraction* that stimulated my interest. Perhaps it is their personality or physical appearance; maybe it is the way they think, their insights, or what they have to say; their artistic, musical gifts; their life experiences, values, or commitments. Most of all I am drawn toward those for whom love, compassion, peace, and justice appear to occupy the core of who they are and the center of their life-focus. There is something that whispers to me, "I'd like to get to know this person better." It draws me toward them and invites further pursuit.
>
> The second aspect to a meaningful relationship for me is *engagement.* An opportunity arises in the moment, or maybe later, for a deeper, more prolonged conversation, or an activity together that affords greater observation.
>
> Sometimes during this time the initial attraction is put off. The other person seems stuck on themselves, has a tendency to mislead by exaggerating or deceiving, or doesn't reciprocate with a corresponding interest in engaging with me. I conclude that my initial attraction was more idealization than reality. I lose interest.
>
> But then there are those moments when that opportunity to get acquainted opens a door even wider

What Makes Our Relationships Meaningful, Satisfying, or Fulfilling?

and provides a fuller perception. It's not that there is always agreement, but there is a healthy, respectful give-and-take, shown in engaged listening, in the asking of questions as if truly interested, and in signs of positive affirmation.

In such exchanges I'm drawn even more toward the person. And something inside me says "I really like this person and I hope we can become better friends." My soul has been touched, not just my eyes and ears. It's more than a surface attraction.

The last aspect of a meaningful relationship for me *is intentionality*. I often sense this early on by how the person engages me. Is there eye contact? Is the person focused in the moment on this time with me, or are they concerned more with what's happening on their phone? Real engagement for me requires that kind of intentionality.

Intentionality, however, also has to do with what happens after an initial engagement. I'm interested in the relationship continuing. Are they? Is there a response to text messages, phone calls, or emails? Do they even initiate some of these? Do they want to get together again, and even take initiative to make this happen? Or does the relationship seem one-sided? For it to last and continue to be meaningful I need to know I'm not the only one engaged in making that happen.

It's amazing. There can be great distance and much time between getting together with a good friend, but in the most meaningful relationships, when that occasion finally happens, it can appear like you are just beginning again where you left off the last time you were together.

That said, it takes work to keep the flame of a good relationship going. Relationships cannot be taken for granted. There must be a deliberate intention that manifests itself in concrete action. But how meaningful when two souls meet, discover and share each other's gifts. Something new is created by that relationship. Both of you are enhanced in ways beyond where you've ever been before. And who knows, this may lead even further,

Making Relationships Meaningful, Satisfying, or Fulfilling

beyond friendship, to the depths of love and a commitment to lifelong partnership.[33]

For additional brief reflections and mini-case studies, see appendix 13.

So, what conclusions may we draw from this study? What do we know, and what don't we know?

CONCLUSIONS

1. As discovered fifty years ago and confirmed in this study, we know that the qualities of communication openness (openness), being oneself (acceptance), and personal support and growth (growth) make our relationships meaningful, satisfying, and fulfilling. While not confirmed in this study, the fourth quality, interpersonal security and warmth, remains a valid and reliable measure and inventory candidate.

   However, it is apparent that the original inventory title, Interpersonal Relationship Satisfaction Inventory (IRSI and IRSI Short Form), is a misnomer. In reality, it is a Meaningful, Satisfying, or Fulfilling Relationships Inventory. From the beginning, we've considered these three constructs jointly rather than individually. In other words, it is not really a "relationship satisfaction" inventory after all; rather, it is a valid and reliable measure of "meaningful, satisfying, or fulfilling relationships." To reflect this more accurate understanding, slight modifications to the inventory title and instructions in the original IRSI and IRSI Short Form are recommended.[34]

---

33. I am grateful to Rev. Al Gephart for his permission to include this extended response; email message to author, September 25, 2025.

34. For example, the inventory can be titled "Meaningful, Satisfying, or Fulfilling Relationships Inventory" or "MSF Relationships Inventory" (Four Qualities). And the original instructions, "Indicate the extent to which you are satisfied with your close personal relationships when considered together as a whole," can now read, "Indicate the extent to which your close personal relationships when considered together as a whole are meaningful, satisfying, or

What Makes Our Relationships Meaningful, Satisfying, or Fulfilling?

You'll find in appendix 9 that the MSF Relationships Inventory (ten themes) measuring the extent to which our relationships are meaningful, satisfying, or fulfilling in the ten thematic areas has made this adjustment. It may also have the flexibility to measure our three constructs jointly as well as individually (more will be said about this flexibility shortly). In any event, if it is used in exploratory or hypothesis-testing research, it needs to be tested for construct validity and reliability.

2. While IRSI may not be a true measure of relationship satisfaction, we can create one based on the features of satisfying relationships we identified in the social science literature in chapter 1. In fact, appendix 14 offers just such a measurement instrument. As you'll see, this new Relationship Satisfaction Inventory (RSI) measures these eight aspects of satisfying relationships: willingness to invest and engage; emotional closeness and affection; experiencing trust and acceptance; experiencing caring and support; having similar or mutual interests; feeling safe and comfortable; talking through and working out arguments and conflict; and communication openness and understanding (see items 1–8). Besides measuring overall relationship satisfaction, you can also measure the satisfaction with each of our four relational qualities (two items per quality) since the eight items happen to fall naturally into our four quality categories. You'll also find that this new inventory measures the extent to which relationships are meaningful, satisfying, and fulfilling (see items 9–11). Instructions for scoring and interpreting results are also provided in appendix 14. Notice also that

fulfilling. Also, "Using a scale of one to six where one is 'not at all, or never' satisfied and six is 'completely, or always' satisfied, please circle the number that best indicates your satisfaction with each aspect of your relationship" can now read, "Using a scale of one to six where one is 'not at all, or never' meaningful, satisfying, or fulfilling and six is 'completely, or always' meaningful, satisfying, or fulfilling. For each aspect of your relationship, please circle the number that best indicates how meaningful, satisfying, or fulfilling it is for you." Finally, the interpretation of results can be adjusted accordingly.

whereas the referent used in the present version is "close personal relationships," other referents may be selected, e.g., personal, friendship, or intimate relationships. And be aware that if the current version is used for exploratory or hypothesis-testing research, it should be tested for construct validity and reliability.

3. Throughout this study we've attempted to define relationships that are meaningful, satisfying, or fulfilling. *Social scientists* have distinctive understandings of each concept, particularly for "meaningful" (having significance, purpose, and coherence) and "fulfilling" (having wellbeing and flourishing). The concept of "satisfying" is less distinct, although it is now operationally defined by the eight features selected for the new RSI (see above). In contrast, *ordinary people* prefer to describe each concept rather than define them. Moreover, their descriptions have more in common[35] than in uniqueness or distinction.[36] And *dictionary definitions*, while distinct for "meaningful" (a state of having purpose or significance), are closely related for "satisfying" (having feelings of enjoyment, pleasure, or contentment) and "fulfilling" (feelings of happiness or satisfaction). Lacking consensus definitions among our three sources, we've chosen to use a "composite definition" for each concept as follows:

- A *meaningful* relationship is one having significance, value, or importance.

- A *satisfying* relationship is one bringing enjoyment, pleasure, or contentment.

- A *fulfilling* relationship is one that thrives or flourishes.

---

35. For example, "mutuality" along with "caring," "loving," and "kind" for "meaningful," "satisfying," and "fulfilling" relationships. Also "trust," "respect," "honesty," and "authenticity"; and "communication" for "meaningful" and "fulfilling" relationships. And "enjoyable," "fun," and "laughter" for "satisfying" and "fulfilling" relationships.

36. In fact, only *acceptance* for "satisfying" relationships, and *comfortable* for "fulfilling" relationships.

What Makes Our Relationships Meaningful, Satisfying, or Fulfilling?

4. In future research on m/s/f relationships, it will be important to decide both how to define m/s/f and who defines m/s/f. If subjects do the defining, then researchers are likely to face the same dilemma as this study: subjects are likely to understand the three constructs differently. We don't know, for example, whether subjects understand m/s/f as either-or or both-and. In other words, are they referring to "meaningful" or "satisfying" or "fulfilling" relationships in their responses, or to "meaningful, and satisfying, and fulfilling" relationships? Or some combination thereof? Or, perhaps, even changing their understanding from question to question?

And let's acknowledge several additional confounding findings from this study. First, m/s/f relationships respondents report that their m/s/f relationships are equally meaningful, satisfying, and fulfilling. Does this give us flexibility to measure our three concepts both jointly, as in this study, and also individually? More specifically, does it mean that we may use both MSF Relationships Inventories (Four Qualities and Ten Themes) to measure our three constructs jointly and individually? In fact, we have done so in this research project. Indeed, participants were divided into three groups, a "meaningful relationships" group, a "satisfying relationships" one, and a "fulfilling relationships" group. We also had both a joint measure of m/s/f (Questionnaire question 1) as well as individual measures (questions 6–8).

And second, respondents may assess their m/s/f relationships differently for different people, in different situations, or at different times in their relationships. They may also value m/s/f relationships differently, perhaps some even higher (or lower) than others, and in varying degrees, situations, and times—and combinations thereof. For example, some of my m/s/f relationships are more important than others, and my satisfying and fulfilling relationships are also meaningful. Complicated, isn't it?

Making Relationships Meaningful, Satisfying, or Fulfilling

While I recommend that future research operationalizes or defines the constructs in similar ways as done in this study, there remains much that we do not yet know about the dynamics of m/s/f relationships.

5. Relationships can be meaningful while not satisfying or fulfilling. For example, I have a meaningful relationship with all 191 of my relatives, friends, good friends, and colleagues. All of these personal relationships are significant, valuable, and important. However, as noted earlier, only around thirty are also satisfying, and around fifty are also fulfilling. My satisfying relationships, those that bring enjoyment, pleasure, or contentment, are mainly among family members, good friends, and colleagues who I see regularly and with whom I experience the relational qualities of openness, acceptance, warmth, and growth. Friends are missing because I do not see most of them regularly. And my fulfilling relationships, those that thrive or flourish, are mainly among family members, friends, and good friends with whom I have ongoing close personal relationships and experience the four relational qualities and many of the ten relational themes. Colleagues are missing because while all are meaningful and some satisfying, our close personal relationships did not continue after we stopped working together (note: a few family members or good friends are also colleagues).

6. Evidence is mounting that relationships are more meaningful and fulfilling than satisfying. Perhaps this growing reality is understandable, especially for fulfilling relationships, since there are nearly twice as many ways that fulfilling relationships are expressed than satisfying ones—three in common (mutuality; caring, loving, and kind; and enjoyable, fun, and laughter) and three additional ways (communication; trust, honesty, respect, and acceptance; and comfortable). Four of these six ways are also included in ways meaningful relationships are experienced (communication; trust, honesty, respect, and authenticity; mutuality; and caring, loving, and kind).

What Makes Our Relationships Meaningful, Satisfying, or Fulfilling?

7. We have learned that participants' relationships as a whole are meaningful, satisfying, and fulfilling. They are also quite healthy overall. In fact, they have significance, value, and importance; they bring enjoyment, pleasure, or contentment; and they thrive and flourish. Perhaps most astonishing, in their m/s/f relationships, they do well on all four qualities and ten themes, including the three descriptors for each quality and theme. Future research is recommended to see if these findings can be replicated.

8. While we've learned which character strengths help create meaningful and fulfilling relationships, and have incorporated these strengths in ways they make relationships m/s/f in this chapter, we don't know how they do so. Likewise, while we've learned that there are wide-ranging features of satisfying relationships, have incorporated them into ways they make relationships m/s/f in this chapter, and have created a new RSI based on them, we don't know how these features make relationships satisfying.

9. Social scientists and ordinary people are both rich sources of wisdom about personal relationships. No doubt we expect expert wisdom and insight from social scientists—after all, it is one of their domains of interest, teaching, research, and community service. We may not, however, give "ordinary people" the credit they deserve. In fact, we may well underestimate or undervalue the depth, diversity, uniqueness, and creativity of their understanding about personal relationships—as reflected in the extraordinary wisdom and insight of their quotations, vignettes, reflections, and case studies.

PRACTICAL APPLICATIONS

1. Review the practical ways we can be open in our communication, be ourselves, experience security and warmth, and experience personal support and growth in our personal

Making Relationships Meaningful, Satisfying, or Fulfilling

relationships. Which ways strike you as particularly wise and useful in making your relationships meaningful, satisfying, or fulfilling? At which ways are you especially adept, and on which can you work to strengthen or enhance the quality of your relationships?

2. Which of the brief quotes for each of the ten themes strike you as particularly wise and useful? How or in what ways can you use them to make your relationships more meaningful, satisfying, or fulfilling?

3. Which of the vignettes for each of the ten relational themes strike you as particularly wise and useful? How or in what ways can you use them to make your relationships more meaningful, satisfying, or fulfilling?

4. Which of the brief reflections and mini-case studies from appendix 13 strike you as particularly wise and useful? How or in what ways can you use them to make your relationships more meaningful, satisfying, or fulfilling?

5. How well does the quotation from Al Gephart summarize how to make our relationships meaningful, satisfying, or fulfilling for you? How or in what ways does this vignette provide a "big-picture" perspective or "integrating" framework for you?

About the Author

THOMAS G. KIRKPATRICK IS an educator, pastor, trainer, writer, and consultant with specialties in interpersonal communication, small group ministries, and conflict management. He is the author of the Roman & Littlefield (Alban) publications *Communication in the Church: A Handbook for Healthier Relationships* and *Small Groups in the Church: A Handbook for Creating Community*, along with the Wipf & Stock publications *Signs of Hope and Health in Mainline Churches: Guidelines for Creating Hopeful and Healthy Congregations* and *Better Ways to Better Relationships in the Church: Guidelines for Practicing Humility, Experiencing Empathy, Feeling Compassion, Showing Kindness, Expressing Appreciation, and Doing Justice*. He has been an adjunct professor at the University of Dubuque Theological Seminary, pastor of Westminster United Presbyterian Church, Galena, Illinois, and interim associate pastor of Little Church on the Prairie Presbyterian Church, Lakewood, Washington. Previously, he was associate professor of speech communication at Whitworth University in Spokane, Washington. He has also served as a campus minister and a program director of camps and conferences. He received his MA and PhD from the University of Washington, DMin from San Francisco Theological Seminary, MDiv from Fuller Theological Seminary, and BMusEd from the University of Oregon. He lives with his wife, also a PCUSA minister, in Maple Valley, Washington, and his four children

About the Author

live in Portland, Oregon; Harrisburg, Oregon; La Crosse, Wisconsin; and Snohomish, Washington.

You can reach him at his website, www.tomkirkpatrick.org.

Appendix 1

Relationship Science
An Overview

THE ACADEMIC DISCIPLINE OF relationship science traces its roots to a meeting of scholars in the summer of 1978. The first major publication was in 1983 by Harold H. Kelly and titled *Close Relationships*. The 2002 version includes 612 pages, 12 chapters, and 9 authors.[1]

As the new introduction puts it, "When the nine of us first met in summer 1978, we were united in our belief that advancement of the scientific study of interpersonal relationships was important to progress in all of the social and behavioral sciences and especially to further progress in our own discipline of psychology. Thus we speak for all of the authors of *Close Relationships* when we express our great pleasure in seeing our book back in print again, for we believe its republication reflects the growing importance of the relationship field."[2]

The further emergence of the field of relationship science is presented in a 1999 article by Ellen Berscheid, "The Greening of

---

1. See Kelley et al., *Close Relationships*. Note: this edition includes a new introduction by Berscheid and Kelley.

2. Kelly et al., *Close Relationships*, vii.

Appendix 1

Relationship Science."[3] Fast-forward to 2013, and here's another summary of the field: "Ellen Berscheid, Elaine Hatfield, and the Emergence of Relationship Science."[4]

The field has two professional journals: *Personal Relationships* (1994–present) and *Journal of Social and Personal Relationships* (1984–present).

Perhaps the best evidence of the maturity of relationship science as an academic discipline is the recent publication of two handbooks of research. First, *The Oxford Handbook of Close Relationships*[5] includes 864 pages, 37 chapters, and 80 authors. See especially chapter 1, "The Blossoming of Relationship Science."

And second, *The Cambridge Handbook of Personal Relationships*[6] includes 596 pages, 40 chapters, and over 100 contributors. See especially chapter 1, "The Seven Seas of the Study of Personal Relationships Research: Historical and Recent Currents," and chapter 40, "Whither Relationship Science? The State of the Science and an Agenda for Moving Forward."[7]

---

3. See Berscheid, "Greening of Relationships Science."

4. See Reis et al., "Ellen Berscheid."

5. See Simpson and Campbell, *Oxford Handbook of Close Relationships*.

6. See Vangelisti and Perlman, *Cambridge Handbook of Personal Relationships*.

7. Here's a sampling of related books: Mashek and Aron, *Handbook of Closeness and Intimacy*; Duck, *Handbook of Personal Relationships*; Fletcher and Fitness, *Knowledge Structures in Close Relationships*; Agnew and Harman, *Power in Close Relationships*; and Pransky, *Relationship Handbook*.

Appendix 2

Research Project Summary
1975

My original research in 1975 began by developing an Interpersonal Relationship Satisfaction Inventory. An initial item pool was generated from three main sources. One source was discussions of two small sharing groups about what makes one's interpersonal relationships meaningful, satisfying, or fulfilling.[1] A second source of items was an upper-division speech communication class of forty students.[2] Third, an extensive literature review produced three somewhat-related measurement instruments[3] and each item was

---

1. Written notes were taken in a four-person sharing group, and a tape recording was used and a transcript made in a five-person sharing group. Individual statements were then extracted from the data and sorted into categories. Categories include interpersonal needs, informality, authenticity, intimacy, helpfulness, supportiveness, and belongingness for one group, and comfortable setting, intimacy (including being oneself and sharing in-depth), personal support, self-identity, and close friendships for the other sharing group.

2. On 3" x 5" index cards students described the variables they perceive to make their relationships meaningful, satisfying, or fulfilling. Statements were then generated from these responses.

3. These include the psychoanalytic, need-oriented Schutz FIRO-B and FIRO-F Scales; the Moos Group Environment Scale Form-R for measuring people's satisfaction with the social climate of groups, families, and teams; and

examined for possible inclusion in the item pool. One hundred fifty-eight items were generated from these three sources.

Four speech communication faculty members and five speech communication graduate students judged the content validity of these items. At the conclusion of this step, one hundred fifty statements were retained for the initial inventory. Sixteen items came from one sharing group, five from the second small group, seventy-eight from speech communication students, and fifty-one from three measurement instruments.

In order to provide both a reasonable time frame for completing the inventory by the anticipated subject pool and also a measure of internal reliability, these one hundred fifty items were randomly ordered and assigned to two separate forms, A and B.

Methods of Initial Testing

The initial inventory was administered to three hundred ordinary people: one hundred eighty students from speech communication classes at the University of Washington, and one hundred twenty church members from Presbyterian Church (USA) congregations in Tacoma, Washington. Half of each sample completed form A and the other half completed form B. All subjects were instructed to indicate to what extent the seventy-five items were true with reference to their closest and most meaningful personal relationships.

Results of Initial Testing

Construct validity was assessed statistically by submitting subject response data to factor analysis. Four factors resulted: "Emotional and Physical Security" (thirty items), "Open Communication"

---

the friendship-model Wright Acquaintance Description Form. The Rogerian-based, growth-oriented Barrett-Lennard Relationship Inventory had not yet been validated and was not included. All four of these measures have been updated and are currently in use by social science researchers. Note: current meaning-oriented, relationship satisfaction, and flourishing relationships conceptualizations and measures will be discussed later.

Research Project Summary

(ten items), "Feeling Fulfilled" (seven items), and "Freedom to Be" (eight items). Since items were randomly assigned to forms A and B, the identical factor structure that resulted in the two forms can be viewed as an informal measure of internal reliability.

Methods of Refinement Testing

The fifty-five remaining items, together with five additional statistically close related items were retained for instrument refinement. These sixty items were assigned to a new form according to a table of random numbers. This new inventory was administered to one hundred seventy-two subjects recruited from experiential small groups (learning groups, expressive groups, or therapy groups) and from undergraduate classes studying interpersonal relationships. These subjects were asked to select one closest and most meaningful personal relationship as a referent for their responses. Since interviews with previous subjects revealed some difficulty in maintaining a consistent referent, it was hoped that greater precision and control over the referent variable would thereby be exercised.

Construct validity was again assessed by submitting the subject response data to factor analysis.[4]

Results of Refinement Testing

As could be expected from item reduction (sixty items instead of one hundred fifty in forms A and B), the new factors had fewer items and there was some item switching among factors in relation to the earlier results. The conceptual interpretation of factors was almost identical to previous findings with the new factor items being even more homogenous. Four new factors resulted labeled "Communication Openness" (eight items), "Personal Support and Growth" (four items), "Being Oneself" (four items), and

---

4. Reliability was assessed by obtaining a measure of the emergent scale's internal consistency using Cronbach's alpha.

Appendix 2

"Interpersonal Security and Warmth" (ten items). An additional fourteen statistically close related items were added, resulting in a new forty-item inventory (see appendix 2).

A global measure of the new forty-item inventory's internal consistency was computed in addition to obtaining reliability coefficients for each of the four scales.[5]

Scoring procedures for the new forty-item inventory are quite simple. An average score for each factor can be computed by totaling the rating numbers (from 1–6) for each item and dividing the total by the number of items for each factor.

---

5. The Cronbach alpha reliability coefficient obtained for all forty items was 0.95. For the eleven-item Communication Openness scale it was 0.90; for the five-item Personal Support and Growth scale it was 0.77; for the nine-item Being Oneself scale it was 0.83; and for the fifteen-item Interpersonal Security and Warmth scale it was 0.92. A questionnaire on referent response behavior revealed that all subjects maintained a consistent referent throughout their responses.

Appendix 3

Interpersonal Relationship Satisfaction Inventory
(IRSI)

INSTRUCTIONS: INDICATE THE EXTENT to which you are satisfied with your close personal relationships when considered together as a whole using a scale of 1–6 where "1" is "not at all, or never" satisfied and "6" is "completely, or always" satisfied. Please circle the number that best indicates your satisfaction with each aspect of your relationship.

In your close personal relationships as a whole, to what extent:	Not At All, Never					Completely, Always
1. Can you share your personal hang-ups?	1	2	3	4	5	6
2. Can you get support in making and living out difficult decisions?	1	2	3	4	5	6
3. Do you gain insight into yourself?	1	2	3	4	5	6

Appendix 3

In your close personal relationships as a whole, to what extent:	Not At All, Never					Completely, Always
4. Do you feel like you're growing and learning?	1	2	3	4	5	6
5. Is something lasting established?	1	2	3	4	5	6
6. Do you feel that you are wanted?	1	2	3	4	5	6
7. Can you discuss family problems?	1	2	3	4	5	6
8. Do you feel energized, excited, and like life is fulfilling?	1	2	3	4	5	6
9. Can you talk about your dreams and ambitions?	1	2	3	4	5	6
10. Can you count on support in any situation?	1	2	3	4	5	6
11. Can you openly disagree?	1	2	3	4	5	6
12. Can you be honest and express your true feelings?	1	2	3	4	5	6
13. Do you feel warmth?	1	2	3	4	5	6
14. Do you have someone to go to in any situation?	1	2	3	4	5	6
15. Do you grow?	1	2	3	4	5	6
16. Are you free to be yourself?	1	2	3	4	5	6
17. Do you respect one another's ideas and opinions?	1	2	3	4	5	6

Interpersonal Relationship Satisfaction Inventory

In your close personal relationships as a whole, to what extent:	Not At All, Never				Completely, Always
18. Do you know that you won't be made fun of should you say something inappropriate or silly?	1	2	3	4	5	6
19. Are basic social needs like security and recognition fulfilled?	1	2	3	4	5	6
20. Can you tell one another about your feelings?	1	2	3	4	5	6
21. Do you invite one another to do things together?	1	2	3	4	5	6
22. Can you express deep emotions?	1	2	3	4	5	6
23. Can you express your inner feelings, thoughts, and goals?	1	2	3	4	5	6
24. Are you able to laugh at yourselves?	1	2	3	4	5	6
25. Are you interested in one another's interests?	1	2	3	4	5	6
26. Can you be both light and serious?	1	2	3	4	5	6
27. Can you talk about those things in your lives which most matter?	1	2	3	4	5	6
28. Do you get a sense of affirmation about yourself?	1	2	3	4	5	6
29. Do you feel truly cared about?	1	2	3	4	5	6
30. Is affection given and received?	1	2	3	4	5	6

Appendix 3

In your close personal relationships as a whole, to what extent:	Not At All, Never					Completely, Always
31. Do you feel important and needed?	1	2	3	4	5	6
32. Is your relationship strong enough to withstand almost any threat to it?	1	2	3	4	5	6
33. Can you open up and express your inner fears and doubts?	1	2	3	4	5	6
34. Can you find help and direction when you're stuck?	1	2	3	4	5	6
35. Are you free from defensiveness?	1	2	3	4	5	6
36. Do you have the opportunity to be yourself?	1	2	3	4	5	6
37. Are you made to feel at ease if you get embarrassed?	1	2	3	4	5	6
38. Could you count on a loan if you were short of cash and needed money in a hurry?	1	2	3	4	5	6
39. Is there sensitivity to one another's needs?	1	2	3	4	5	6
40. Do you experience emotional security?	1	2	3	4	5	6

Scoring—Add circled numbers for items in each relational quality and divide total by number of items to arrive at an average rating for each quality:

Communication Openness—11 items (1, 7, 9, 12, 14, 20, 22, 23, 27, 33, 34)
    Divide total score by 11 and enter average here: _____

Interpersonal Relationship Satisfaction Inventory

Being Oneself—9 items (11, 16, 17, 24, 25, 26, 35, 36, 37)
    Divide total score by 9 and enter average here: _____

Interpersonal Security and Warmth—15 items (5, 6, 8, 13, 18, 19, 21, 28, 29, 30, 31, 32, 38, 39, 40)
    Divide total score by 15 and enter average here: _____

Personal Support and Growth—5 items (2, 3, 4, 10, 15)
    Divide total score by 5 and enter average here: _____

Interpreting Results—Consider scores of 5 or 6 as "very satisfied" or "high" ratings, 3 or 4 as "moderately satisfied" or "average" ratings, and 1 or 2 as "not very satisfied" or "low" ratings.

Appendix 4

Interpersonal Relationship Satisfaction Inventory
(IRSI Short Form)

INSTRUCTIONS: INDICATE THE EXTENT to which you are satisfied with your close personal relationships when considered together as a whole using a scale of 1–6 where "1" is "not at all, or never" satisfied and "6" is "completely, or always" satisfied. Please circle the number that best indicates your satisfaction with each aspect of your relationship.

In your close personal relationships as a whole, to what extent:	Not At All, Never					Completely, Always
1. Can you share your personal problems?	1	2	3	4	5	6
2. Do you gain insight into yourself?	1	2	3	4	5	6
3. Do you feel like you're growing and learning?	1	2	3	4	5	6

Interpersonal Relationship Satisfaction Inventory

In your close personal relationships as a whole, to what extent:	Not At All, Never					Completely, Always
4. Do you feel that you're wanted?	1	2	3	4	5	6
5. Can you grow?	1	2	3	4	5	6
6. Do you respect one another's ideas and opinions?	1	2	3	4	5	6
7. Can you tell one another about your feelings?	1	2	3	4	5	6
8. Are you able to laugh at yourselves?	1	2	3	4	5	6
9. Do you feel truly cared about?	1	2	3	4	5	6
10. Do you feel important and needed?	1	2	3	4	5	6
11. Can you open up and express your doubts and fears?	1	2	3	4	5	6
12. Do you have the opportunity to be yourself?	1	2	3	4	5	6

Scoring—Add circled numbers for three items in each relational quality and divide total by three to arrive at an average rating for each quality:

Communication Openness—3 items (1, 7, 11)
        Divide total score by 3 and enter average here: _____

Being Oneself—3 items (6, 8, 12)
        Divide total score by 3 and enter average here: _____

Interpersonal Security and Warmth—3 items (4, 9, 10)
        Divide total score by 3 and enter average here: _____

Appendix 4

Personal Support and Growth—3 items (2, 3, 5)
    Divide total score by 3 and enter average here: _____

Interpreting Results—Consider scores of 5 or 6 as "very satisfied" or "high" ratings, 3 or 4 as "moderately satisfied" or "average" ratings, and 1 or 2 as "not very satisfied" or "low" ratings.

Appendix 5

Four C's Signs of Relational Health

Community—Ways We Share with One Another

- Building relationships
- Affirming and supporting
- Experiencing trust
- Showing empathy
- Practicing forgiveness
- Bridging cultures

Communication—Ways We Interact with One Another

- Engaging conflict
- Listening attentively
- Finding common ground
- Technologically savvy

Appendix 5

- Expressing appreciation
- Exercising curiosity

Character—Ways We Treat One Another

- Doing justice
- Showing kindness
- Practicing humility
- Feeling compassion
- Demonstrating love
- Promoting peace

Collaboration—Ways We Work with One Another

- Strategizing and visioning
- Discerning and decision-making
- Openness to change
- Organizational agility
- Engagement of spiritual gifts
- Partnering

Appendix 6

Meaningful, Satisfying, or Fulfilling Relationships Themes
(Percent and Number of Respondents)

Respondents 66 Percent (126 of 191)

Family Members 73 Percent (41 of 56)

- Connection (19)
- Communication (18)
- Time (17)
- Enjoyment (16)
- Being Oneself/Known (13)
- Mutuality (12)
- Presence (10)
- Transcendence (8)

- Valued (8)
- Work (7)
- Growth (3)

Friends 63 Percent (31 of 49)

- Connection (13)
- Being Oneself/Known (13)
- Time (13)
- Mutuality (11)
- Communication (10)
- Enjoyment (10)
- Work (6)
- Presence (5)
- Growth (5)
- Valued (3)

Good Friends 64 Percent (9 of 14)

- Communication (7)
- Connection (5)
- Mutuality (5)
- Time (6)
- Enjoyment (4)
- Being Oneself/Known (4)
- Work (3)
- Support and Growth (2)

Meaningful, Satisfying, or Fulfilling Relationships Themes

Colleagues 63 Percent (45 of 72)

Clergypersons 64 Percent (27 of 42)

- Mutuality (19)
- Connection (16)
- Enjoyment (16)
- Communication (11)
- Growth (9)
- Transcendence (7)
- Being Oneself/Known (6)
- Time (5)
- Work (5)
- Presence (3)

Laypersons 60 Percent (18 of 30)

- Connection (11)
- Enjoyment (10)
- Mutuality (9)
- Communication (7)
- Being Oneself/Known (6)
- Time (5)
- Transcendence (3)
- Growth (2)
- Presence (2)

Appendix 6

TOTALS—3 Themes/Respondent (397 Responses from 126 Respondents)

- Connection 51 percent (64)
- Mutuality 44 percent (56)
- Enjoyment 44 percent (56)
- Communication 42 percent (53)

———————————

- Time 37 percent (46)
- Being Oneself/Known 33 percent (42)

———————————

- Growth 17 percent (21)
- Work 17 percent (21)
- Presence 16 percent (20)
- Transcendence 14 percent (18)

Appendix 7

Theme-Related Word Usage
(Percent and Number of Respondent Word Usage)

N = 126
Love 30 percent (38)
Respect 25 percent (31)
Life 25 percent (31)
Together 25 percent (31)

———————————

Listen 23 percent (29)
Differences 21 percent (27)
Trust 20 percent (25)
Value 20 percent (25)
Caring 18 percent (23)
Honesty 17 percent (21)
Interests 17 percent (21)

———————————

Spiritual/Faith 15 percent (19)
Kindness 14 percent (18)
Understanding 14 percent (17)
Conversation 14 percent (17)
Belief 11 percent (14)

Appendix 7

Support 10 percent (13)
Challenges 10 percent (13)
Laughter 10 percent (12)
Humor 10 percent (12)
Emotional 10 percent (12)
God 9 percent (11)
Comfortable 9 percent (11)
Similarities 9 percent (11)
Commitment 8 percent (10)
Vulnerable 8 percent (10)
Positive 8 percent (10)

Others: Sharing (9), Joy (9), Partner (9), Intentional (7), Space (7), Compassion (7), Reciprocal (7), Goals (7), Change (7), Fun (7), Community (6), Equal (6), Rewarding (6), Pray (6), Impact (5), Intimacy (5), Problems (5), Jesus (5), Integrity (5), Gratitude (5), Play (5), Bonds (5), Soul (5), Attention (4), Positivity (4), Forgiveness (4), Initiative (4), Effort (4), Authentic (4), Truth (4), Adventure (4), Surprise (4), Diversity (4), Empathy (4), Humility (3), Culture (3), Collaborative (3), Purpose (3), Encourage (3), Affirm (3), Nurture (3), Gifts (3), Patience (3), Affection (3), Loyalty (3), Courage (2), Belonging (2), Intellectual (2), Backgrounds (2), Sympathize (2), Impact (2), Inclusive (2), Passion (2), Hugs (2), Risk (2), Chemistry (2), Bible (2), Wellbeing (2), and Engaged (2).

Appendix 8

Meaningful, Satisfying, or Fulfilling Relationships Themes Components

CONNECTION

WAYS PEOPLE CONNECT WITH one another—attention, trust, respect, loyalty, brave space, sharing, caring, support, collaboration, partnering, deep friendship, belonging, chemistry, "clicking," intimacy, affection, vulnerability, positive sexuality, bonding, love, empathy, sympathizing, kindness, compassion, humility, appreciation, bridging cultures, togetherness, and community.

MUTUALITY

Ways people have mutual interests—similarities, backgrounds, cultural differences, beliefs, values, goals, lifestyles, purpose, impact, reciprocity, shared understanding, shared experience, sharing real life, giving and receiving love, empathy, diversity, inclusiveness, and equality.

Appendix 8

ENJOYMENT

Ways people enjoy being with one another—playing, having fun, laughter, humor, love of life, beauty, surprise, awe, wonder, appreciation, camaraderie, novelty, adventure, rewarding, showing up, comfortable, passion, affection, holding hands, hugs, remembering, positivity, and gratitude.

COMMUNICATION

Ways people communicate with one another—deep and quality conversation, openness, sharing, listening, being understood, trust and risk, honesty, empathy, truthfulness, phone, email, texting, face-to-face, showing love through gestures, speech, and deeds.

TIME

Ways people spend time together—taking initiative to be together, being together in silence, being comfortable, intentionally present, deep conversation transcends time, adapt to seasons of life, picking up right where you left off after an absence, and bridging distances.

BEING ONESELF/KNOWN

Ways people feel free to be themselves—acceptance, attention, courage, authenticity, genuineness, safe space, comfortable, being understood, trust and risk, respect, integrity, sharing real life, encouragement, affirmation, being valued, nurturing, vulnerable, unconditional love, empathy, and patience.

GROWTH

Ways people learn and grow—challenges, commitment, accountability, emotional intelligence, taking initiative, openness to

Meaningful, Satisfying, or Fulfilling Relationships Themes Components

change, courage, taking risks, vulnerability, humility, gifts, creating space for growth, differences promote growth and learning, practicing forgiveness, support, nurture, encouragement, promoting wellbeing, navigating obstacles, setting goals, adapting and evolving, solving problems, and impacting one another's lives—moving through the world differently after positive encounters.

WORK

Ways people work at their relationships—face and overcome obstacles, problem-solve, take initiative, be intentional, humility, patience, commitment, set and keep boundaries, accept differences, let go, and practice forgiveness.

PRESENCE

Ways people are present and available—attentive, showing up, sharing and listening, understanding, caring, intentional, value, respect, impact, bonds, initiative, loyalty, together, belonging, comfortable, hugs, and effort.

TRANSCENDENCE

Ways people feed their soul and spirit—Spirit, God, Jesus, faith, hope, love, beliefs, spiritual guidance, imminent divinity, truth, Bible, gifts, prayer, life together, worship, attunement with nature, and soul friends.

Appendix 9

MSF Relationships Inventory
(Ten Themes)

INSTRUCTIONS: INDICATE THE EXTENT to which your relationships are meaningful, satisfying, or fulfilling in the ten areas listed below using a scale of 1–6 where "1" is "not at all, or never" and "6" is "completely, or always." Please circle the number that best indicates your response to each area of your relationship.

To what extent are your relationships meaningful, satisfying, or fulfilling in the following areas:	Not At All, Never					Completely, Always
1. Ways you connect with one another	1	2	3	4	5	6
2. Ways you have mutual interests	1	2	3	4	5	6
3. Ways you enjoy being with one another	1	2	3	4	5	6
4. Ways you communicate with one another	1	2	3	4	5	6

MSF Relationships Inventory

To what extent are your relationships meaningful, satisfying, or fulfilling in the following areas:	Not At All, Never					Completely, Always
5. Ways you spend time together	1	2	3	4	5	6
6. Ways you feel free to be yourself	1	2	3	4	5	6
7. Ways you learn and grow	1	2	3	4	5	6
8. Ways you work at your relationship	1	2	3	4	5	6
9. Ways you are present and available	1	2	3	4	5	6
10. Ways you feed your soul and spirit	1	2	3	4	5	6

Interpreting Results—Consider scores of 5 or 6 as "very meaningful, satisfying, or fulfilling" or "high" ratings, 3 or 4 as "moderately meaningful, satisfying, or fulfilling" or "average" ratings, and 1 or 2 as "not very meaningful, satisfying, or fulfilling" or "low" ratings.

Appendix 10

Meaningful, Satisfying, and Fulfilling Word Usage
(Percent and Number of Respondent Word Usage)

Relationship(s) 2 times/respondent (258 times from 126 respondents)

Meaningful 46 percent (82 times by 58 respondents, standalone by 17 respondents)

Satisfying 28 percent (48 times by 35 respondents, standalone by 18 respondents)

Fulfilling 24 percent (40 times by 30 respondents, standalone by 11 respondents)

Meaningful, Satisfying, and Fulfilling Word Usage

Meaningful Relationship(s) 14 percent (17)

Satisfying Relationship(s) 5 percent (6)

Fulfilling Relationship(s) 2 percent (2)

Meaningful, Satisfying, and Fulfilling Relationships 5 percent (6)

Appendix 11

Questionnaire Questions

1. What one or two words or phrases best define a *m/s/f* relationship for you?

2. How many m/s/f relationships do you have [3 or fewer, 4–10, 10–30, 30–60, 60–100, 100–200, more than 200]?

3. Among what type of personal relationships are most of your m/s/f relationships (you may select more than one answer)[1] [family members, friends, good friends, colleagues, or several of the above]?

4. In your relationships as a whole, to what extent do you find them m/s/f? [using a scale of 1 to 6 where 1 equals never or very little and 6 equals always or very much]

---

1. Meaningful Relationship Questionnaire and Satisfying Relationship Questionnaire respondents could select more than one answer. However, a Google Forms technical glitch prevented Fulfilling Relationship Questionnaire respondents from doing so. Hence, results for the "several of the above" answer option are skewed for these respondents and will be noted in the results accordingly.

Questionnaire Questions

5. How do you rate the overall health of your m/s/f relationships [using a scale of 1 to 6 where 1 equals very poor and 6 equals excellent]?
6. In your m/s/f relationships, to what extent do they have significance, value, or importance to you [using a scale of 1 to 6 where 1 equals never or very little and 6 equals always or very much]?
7. In your m/s/f relationships, to what extent do they bring you enjoyment, pleasure, or contentment [same as previous scale]?
8. In your m/s/f relationships, to what extent do they thrive or flourish [same scale]?
9. In your m/s/f relationships, to what extent can you be open in your communication [same scale]? In particular, how well can you do the following:
    a. Open up and express your doubts and fears [1 equals not well and 6 equals very well]?
    b. Tell one another about your feelings [same as previous scale]?
    c. Share your personal problems [same scale]?
10. In your m/s/f relationships, to what extent can you be yourselves? In particular, how well do you do the following: [same scales]
    a. Respect one another's ideas and opinions?
    b. Be able to laugh at yourselves?
    c. Experience trust and empathy with one another?
11. In your m/s/f relationships, to what extent do you experience interpersonal security and warmth? In particular, how well do you do the following: [same scales]
    a. Feel that you are valued and wanted?
    b. Feel affection and care for one another?

c. Feel important to and safe with one another?

12. In your m/s/f relationships, to what extent do you experience personal support and growth? In particular, how well do you do the following: [same scales]

    a. Gain insight into yourself?

    b. Feel like you are growing and learning?

    c. Feel supported by one another?

13. In your m/s/f relationships, to what extent do you connect with one another? In particular, how well do you connect with one another in the following ways: [same scales]

    a. Belonging and togetherness?

    b. Having chemistry and "clicking" with one another?

    c. Giving attention to and expressing appreciation for one another?

14. In your m/s/f relationships, to what extent do you have mutual interests? In particular, how well do your mutual interests show up in the following ways: [same scales]

    a. Common beliefs and values?

    b. Respect and reciprocity?

    c. Shared understanding and experiences?

15. In your m/s/f relationships, to what extent do you enjoy being with one another? In particular, how well do you enjoy one another in the following ways: [same scales]

    a. Camaraderie and a spirit of adventure?

    b. Lightheartedness and fun-loving?

    c. Bonds of warmth and affection?

16. In your m/s/f relationships, to what extent do you communicate well with one another? In particular, how well do you communicate in the following ways: [same scales]

    a. Free-flowing and ease of conversation?

b. Listening and being understood?

   c. Honesty and authenticity?

17. In your m/s/f relationships, to what extent do you spend time together? In particular, how well do you spend time together in the following ways: [same scales]

    a. Taking initiative to be together?

    b. At ease with silence?

    c. Picking up right where you left off after an absence?

18. In your m/s/f relationships, to what extent are you free to be yourselves? In particular, how well are you free to be yourselves in the following ways: [same scales]

    a. Acceptance and affirmation?

    b. Vulnerability and safety?

    c. Genuineness and integrity?

19. In your m/s/f relationships, to what extent do you learn and grow? In particular, how well do you learn and grow in the following ways: [same scales]

    a. Openness to change?

    b. Welcome challenges and differences?

    c. Nurture and support one another?

20. In your m/s/f relationships, to what extent do you work at your relationships? In particular, how well do you work at your relationships in the following ways: [same scales]

    a. Facing and overcoming obstacles in your relationships?

    b. Setting and keeping boundaries?

    c. Letting go and practicing forgiveness as appropriate?

21. In your m/s/f relationships, to what extent are you present and available to one another? In particular, how well are you present and available to one another in the following ways: [same scales]

Appendix 11

    a. Showing up and being attentive?

    b. Feeling comfortable with one another?

    c. Feeling valued and respected?

22. In your m/s/f relationships, to what extent do you feed your souls and spirits? In particular, how well do you feed your soul and spirit in the following ways: [same scales]

    a. Connecting to something greater than yourself?

    b. Participating in religious or spiritual rituals or practices?

    c. Creating a sense of community or soul friendships?

Appendix 12

Questionnaires Results
N = 80

1. What one or two words or phrases best define a *m/s/f* relationship for you?

Meaningful Relationships

N = 28

Trust, respect, honesty, and authenticity = 17

Mutuality = 7

Love and care = 7

Communication = 7

Plus satisfying, affirming, empathy, sincerity, dependability, being known, building each other up

Appendix 12

Satisfying Relationships

N = 24

Acceptance (being known, openness, intimate, vulnerability, heard and seen, comfortable, empathy, safe, understanding, excited to see, interest in being together) = 16

Mutuality (growth, interest, reciprocal, shared beliefs and interests and values, connect, friendship, compatibility, history together) = 12

Respect = 5

Enjoyable, fun, humor, laugh together = 5

Caring, loving, kind = 4

Plus growth, collaborative, dependable

Note: no communication or trust

Fulfilling Relationships

N = 28

Trust, honesty, respect, acceptance = 16

Comfortable (partnership, quality time, shared commitments, thankful, tending to one another, resonant, peaceful, intimacy, vulnerability, intentional and unconditional) = 12

Mutuality (support, respect, reciprocal, intentional and unconditional) = 7

Care, love, kind, empathy, sacrificial = 7

Communication = 3

Enjoyment, fun, laughter = 3

Questionnaires Results

2. How many m/s/f relationships with people do you have?

Questionnaire	Meaningful	Satisfying	Fulfilling	Average
	n = 28	n = 24	n = 28	n = 80
3 or fewer	3 (10 %)	1 (4 %)	4 (4 %)	8 (10 %)
4–10	9 (32 %)	9 (38 %)	13 (46 %)	31 (39 %)
10–30	13 (46 %)	9 (38 %)	9 (32 %)	31 (39 %)
30–60	3 (10 %)	3 (13 %)	1 (3 %)	7 (9 %)
60–100	0	2 (8 %)	0	2 (2.5 %)
100–200	0	0	0	0
More than 200	0	0	1 (3 %)	1 (1 %)

3. Among what type of personal relationships are most of your m/s/f relationships (you may select more than one answer)?

Questionnaire	Meaningful	Satisfying	Fulfilling	Total
	n = 28	n = 24	n = 28	n = 80
Family Members	18 (64 %)	14 (61 %)	12 (43 %)	44 (55 %)
Friends	4 (14 %)	4 (17 %)	1 (4 %)	9 (11 %)
Good Friends	17 (61 %)	15 (65 %)	2 (7 %)	34 (43 %)
Colleagues	3 (11 %)	6 (26 %)	0	9 (11 %)
Several of the Above	9 (32 %)	6 (26 %)	13 (46 %)	28 (35 %)

4. In your relationships as a whole, to what extent do you find them m/s/f?

Questionnaire	Meaningful	Satisfying	Fulfilling	Combined
	n = 28	n = 24	n = 28	n = 80
Average (1 to 6)	4.96	4.4	4.86	4.74

Appendix 12

5. How do you rate the overall health of your m/s/f?

Questionnaire	Meaningful	Satisfying	Fulfilling	Combined
	n = 28	n = 24	n = 28	n = 80
Average (1 to 6)	5.15	4.96	4.9	5.0

6. In your m/s/f relationships, to what extent do they have significance, value, or importance to you?

Questionnaire	Meaningful	Satisfying	Fulfilling	Combined
	n = 28	n = 24	n = 28	n = 80
Average (1 to 6)	5.7	5.5	5.8	5.7

7. In your m/s/f relationships, to what extent do they bring you enjoyment, pleasure, or contentment?

Questionnaire	Meaningful	Satisfying	Fulfilling	Combined
	n = 28	n = 24	n = 28	n = 80
Average (1 to 6)	5.3	5.4	5.4	5.4

8. In your m/s/f relationships, to what extent do they thrive or flourish?

Questionnaire	Meaningful	Satisfying	Fulfilling	Combined
	n = 28	n = 24	n = 28	n = 80
Average (1 to 6)	5.4	4.3	4.9	4.9

Questionnaires Results

9. In your m/s/f relationships, to what extent can you be open in your communication?

Questionnaire	Meaningful	Satisfying	Fulfilling	Combined
	n = 28	n = 24	n = 28	n = 80
Average (1 to 6)	5.2	4.96	4.9	5.0
a. Open up and express your doubts and fears?	4.5	4.5	4.6	4.5
b. Tell one another about your feelings?	4.6	4.6	4.7	4.6
c. Share your personal problems?	4.6	4.8	4.8	4.7

10. In your m/s/f relationships, to what extent can you be yourselves?

Questionnaire	Meaningful	Satisfying	Fulfilling	Combined
	n = 28	n = 24	n = 28	n = 80
Average (1 to 6)	5.2	4.96	4.9	5.0
a. Respect one another's ideas and opinions?	5.4	5.3	5.4	5.4
b. Be able to laugh at yourselves?	5.5	5.4	5.2	5.4
c. Experience trust and empathy with one another?	5.4	5.5	5.4	5.4

Appendix 12

11. In your m/s/f relationships, to what extent do you experience interpersonal security and warmth?

Questionnaire	Meaningful	Satisfying	Fulfilling	Combined
	n = 28	*n = 24*	*n = 28*	*n = 80*
Average (1 to 6)	5.2	5.2	5.2	5.2
a. Feel that you are valued and wanted?	5.2	5.2	5.1	5.2
b. Feel affection and care for one another?	5.3	5.4	5.4	5.4
c. Feel important to and safe with one another?	5.4	5.4	5.4	5.4

12. In your m/s/f relationships, to what extent do you experience personal support and growth?

Questionnaire	Meaningful	Satisfying	Fulfilling	Combined
	n = 28	*n = 24*	*n = 28*	*n = 80*
Average (1 to 6)	5.2	5.25	5.1	5.2
a. Gain insight into yourself?	5.1	4.65	5.1	5.0
b. Feel you are growing and learning?	5.25	5.3	5.2	5.25
c. Feel supported by one another?	5.2	5.3	5.3	5.3

Questionnaires Results

13. In your m/s/f relationships, to what extent do you connect with one another?

Questionnaire	Meaningful	Satisfying	Fulfilling	Combined
	$n = 28$	$n = 24$	$n = 28$	$n = 80$
Average (1 to 6)	5.0	5.1	5.0	5.0
a. Belonging and togetherness?	5.0	5.0	5.2	5.1
b. Have chemistry and "clicking" with one another?	5.0	4.8	5.1	5.0
c. Giving attention to and expressing appreciation for one another?	5.3	5.2	5.2	5.2

14. In your m/s/f relationships, to what extent do you have mutual interests?

Questionnaire	Meaningful	Satisfying	Fulfilling	Combined
	$n = 28$	$n = 24$	$n = 28$	$n = 80$
Average (1 to 6)	4.9	4.9	4.8	4.9
a. Common beliefs and values?	4.9	5.1	4.96	5.0
b. Respect and reciprocity?	5.3	5.4	5.4	5.4

Appendix 12

Questionnaire	Meaningful	Satisfying	Fulfilling	Combined
c. Shared understanding and experiences?	4.7	4.9	5.1	4.9

15. In your m/s/f relationships, to what extent do you enjoy being with one another?

Questionnaire	Meaningful	Satisfying	Fulfilling	Combined
	$n = 28$	$n = 24$	$n = 28$	$n = 80$
Average (1 to 6)	5.6	5.5	5.6	5.6
a. Camaraderie and a spirit of adventure?	4.6	4.7	5.1	4.8
b. Lightheartedness and fun-loving?	5.2	4.9	4.8	5.0
c. Bonds of warmth and affection?	5.2	5.2	5.25	5.2

16. In your m/s/f relationships, to what extent do you communicate well with one another?

Questionnaire	Meaningful	Satisfying	Fulfilling	Combined
	$n = 28$	$n = 24$	$n = 28$	$n = 80$
Average (1 to 6)	5.0	4.96	4.8	4.9

Questionnaires Results

Questionnaire	Meaningful	Satisfying	Fulfilling	Combined
a. Free-flowing and ease of conversation?	5.1	5.0	5.25	5.1
b. Listening and being understood?	5.1	5.1	4.7	5.0
c. Honesty and authenticity?	5.4	5.3	4.8	5.2

17. In your m/s/f relationships, to what extent do you spend time together?

Questionnaire	Meaningful	Satisfying	Fulfilling	Combined
	n = 28	n = 24	n = 28	n = 80
Average (1 to 6)	4.3	4.4	4.7	4.5
a. Taking initiative to be together?	4.5	4.5	4.8	4.6
b. At ease with silence?	4.9	5.0	4.6	4.8
c. Picking up right where you left off after an absence?	5.5	5.3	5.3	5.4

18. In your m/s/f relationships, to what extent are you free to be yourselves?

Questionnaire	Meaningful	Satisfying	Fulfilling	Combined
	n = 28	n = 24	n = 28	n = 80

Appendix 12

Questionnaire	Meaningful	Satisfying	Fulfilling	Combined
Average (1 to 6)	5.4	5.2	5.4	5.3
a. Acceptance and affirmation?	5.2	5.1	5.1	5.1
b. Vulnerability and safety?	5.5	5.1	5.4	5.3
c. Genuineness and integrity?	5.7	5.7	5.4	5.6

19. In your m/s/f relationships, to what extent do you learn and grow?

Questionnaire	Meaningful	Satisfying	Fulfilling	Combined
	n = 28	n = 24	n = 28	n = 80
Average (1 to 6)	5.4	4.7	5.1	5.1
a. Openness to change?	5.0	4.6	4.75	4.8
b. Welcome challenges and differences?	4.9	4.7	4.9	4.8
c. Nurture and support one another?	5.3	5.5	5.3	5.4

20. In your m/s/f relationships, to what extent do you work at your relationships?

Questionnaire	Meaningful	Satisfying	Fulfilling	Combined
	n = 28	n = 24	n = 28	n = 80

Questionnaires Results

Questionnaire	Meaningful	Satisfying	Fulfilling	Combined
Average (1 to 6)	4.9	4.75	4.8	4.8
a. Facing and overcoming obstacles in your relationships?	4.7	4.7	4.6	4.7
b. Setting and keeping boundaries?	4.4	4.6	4.75	4.6
c. Letting go and practicing forgiveness as appropriate?	5.2	4.8	4.9	5.0

21. In your m/s/f relationships, to what extent are you present and available to one another?

Questionnaire	Meaningful	Satisfying	Fulfilling	Combined
	n = 28	n = 24	n = 28	n = 80
Average (1 to 6)	5.1	4.9	5.1	5.1
a. Showing up and being attentive?	5.1	5.0	5.1	5.1
b. Feeling comfortable with one another?	5.4	5.3	5.0	5.2
c. Feeling valued and respected?	5.4	5.25	5.3	5.3

Appendix 12

22. In your m/s/f relationships, to what extent do you feed your souls and spirits?

Questionnaire	Meaningful	Satisfying	Fulfilling	Total
	n = 28	n = 24	n = 28	n = 80
Average (1 to 6)	4.7	4.8	5.1	4.9
a. Connecting to something greater than yourself?	4.6	4.9	4.9	4.8
b. Participating in religious or spiritual rituals or practices?	3.9	4.5	4.5	4.3
c. Creating a sense of community or soul friendships?	4.8	4.4	4.75	4.65

Appendix 13

Brief Reflections and Mini-Case Studies

BRIEF REFLECTIONS

My relationships that are meaningful, satisfying, and fulfilling stem from deep love and respect for one another, an alignment of values, an ability to enjoy life, an openness to new things, and a willingness to put in the work to make things better.[1]

* * *

Relationships are meaningful because they:
- Change our perspective.
- Bear witness to our feelings, ideas, and challenges.
- Lift our mood.
- Give a sense of belonging.
- Facilitate growth.
- Make us feel heard and seen.[2]

---

1. Email message to author, September 24, 2025.
2. Email message to author, September 24, 2025.

Appendix 13

* * *

A meaningful relationship has a shared interest, passion, or value.

A satisfying relationship is safe; there is no judgment, and there is equality.

A fulfilling relationship has genuine mutual affection. "I like you and you like me."[3]

* * *

In contemplating your question I realized that my response would be the same for meaningful, satisfying, and fulfilling relationships.
- Shared common interests which includes faith, family, and friends
- Duration and shared life experiences
- Adaptations and evolving as we age[4]

* * *

Meaningful . . . Those people with whom we share a common set of values and faith.

Satisfying . . . Watching our children raise their own children.

Fulfilling . . . Friends and family that have thirst for knowledge and share their experiences.[5]

* * *

Meaningful relationships change you, affirm you in healthy ways, and give you the opportunity to affirm or speak into what you see in others positively.

Satisfying relationships center on shared understanding, either from common experiences or from common ground gained through knowing each other.

Fulfilling relationships connect different experiences to my own experience—not simply being known

---

3. Email message to author, September 24, 2025.
4. Email message to author, September 24, 2025.
5. Email message to author, September 25, 2025.

Brief Reflections and Mini-Case Studies

and loved, but also moving through the world differently as a result.[6]

* * *

Meaningful relationships involve shared purpose (this can be faith, mission, employment, etc.).

Satisfying relationships make me feel better both anticipating and sharing time together.

Fulfilling relationships means knowing that we care for one another.[7]

* * *

What makes my relationships meaningful, satisfying, or fulfilling? I would say intentionality, hard work, love, surprise, and change. By "intentionality" I mean expending the effort to connect with someone on a deep level, to get to know them and make myself known. That doesn't just happen; it takes hard work. I'm talking about the hard work of leaning in rather than turning away when irked or even when disinterested because of lack of understanding. It means being willing to sacrifice in order to be there for the other. It means going out of my way to accommodate the needs to the other. Now, I guess I am getting dangerously close to some of the definitions of love—love being defined so wonderfully in Rom 12 and 1 Cor 13. I always find love full of surprises, because when I have been brave enough to love someone, truly, whether a sister, a friend, an advocate, or adversary, I am often surprised by joy, an astounding learning or insight, or humor. And, of course, it is always the surprise of love that calls me to change my deepest understandings of someone, or myself, or the world.[8]

* * *

These three things make relationships meaningful to me:

6. Email message to author, September 24, 2025.
7. Email message to author, September 24, 2025.
8. Email message to author, September 24, 2025.

Appendix 13

1. Mutual respect and trust: it's OK to have differences, but be respectful when you differ and open to hearing other points of view. Furthermore, be respectful of each other's time and be present when we're together. Being able to trust one another is extremely important to me. There are always circumstances that will push these boundaries, so having the full trust of your partner or friend is so important.
2. Similarities: having similar interests is important in my relationships. With my spouse and close friends, both have very similar interests and enjoy spending time doing those interests together. Having similar parenting ideals is also very meaningful. I find that having friends raise their kids with similar standards to how they behave as we do makes it fun and easy to be around.
3. Communication and honesty: being able to communicate openly in relationships is crucial to having them be lasting ones. This is something I am constantly working on to be better at, but I know it's important and I value it. So many relationships are ruined over miscommunication or misunderstanding, so it's best to always be honest and truthful with your intentions and feelings.

In the end, with how little free time I have, I try to make those moments count and am picky about who I share my time with. I feel very lucky to have such great relationships surrounding me and my family![9]

* * *

What makes a meaningful relationship with another person? For me, it must be based on a firm foundation of trust, mutual respect, and total honesty. With these in place as key building blocks I can feel comfortable to share my feelings, opinions, and intimate thoughts with the other person and risk letting my wall of self-protection to come down.

---

9. Email message to author, September 24, 2025.

Brief Reflections and Mini-Case Studies

Another critical element to a lasting relationship is being a good listener. To be truly listened to, understood, and not feel judged or criticized is a priceless gift one person can give to another person. This then gives me the freedom and confidence to know that I can call that person anytime, in any situation, and know they will be there for me, knowing they only want the best for me.

Building a deep and valued relationship cannot be rushed; it takes time but the rewards are priceless. You have created a friendship that has made your life fuller, richer, and more meaningful by having that person in it.[10]

MINI-CASE STUDIES

Mutuality

I've learned something about myself the last ten or so years through dysfunctional or failed relationships and friendships (both familial and "friends"), that one of the most important things to me is a genuine, mutual interest in having a relationship with one another. Both people have to care to maintain the relationship. Sometimes one party will put in more than 50 percent of the effort to do so; other times the other party will. Most of the time it will be a natural ebb and flow; other times it will be out of necessity. But averaged out over the long-term, if it's important enough to both parties, they will both make it a priority to put in the effort to make it work.[11]

Friendships

I grew up struggling to keep close friendships, and I worked very hard to be someone people wanted to be

---

10. Email message to author, September 25, 2025.
11. Email message to author, September 24, 2025.

close to: pretty, fun, confident, a leader. That's what I thought someone would want in a friend. The attributes changed as I got older: smart, cool, funny, quirky, and talented. I had to mold myself to be those things in order to be interesting, lovable, and worthy of my friendships. And it wasn't just friends; it extended to my relationships with my family and dating. It wasn't until I was in my twenties did that begin to change. I have one particular friend that I have known since middle school, who I used to deem as not as "cool" as my other friends. But she was funny and seemed to really like and care about me when I felt forgotten by other friends. And over the years, I've come to find that relationship far more meaningful than any other friendship I'd experienced before. We were roommates in college, and every day she showed me unconditional love. We took care of each other, supported each other's talents and interests, were honest with each other when something was wrong, and often knew each other better than our families. It was the intimacy of being known and loved and cared for that was so fulfilling. It's when being with that person feels like a safe harbor from everything else and they remind you who you are and how amazing and capable you are. She was an example of true Christlike love to me. From that friendship I learned that I was lovable and what I needed to look for in my other relationships. I ended up meeting other friends who felt the same way about me. We have a shared sense of humor, we prioritize quality time and deep conversation, and make an effort to keep the relationship alive and vibrant, even when distance divides us. Keeping long-distance friendships can be hard, and not all of them will be the kind you can count on. But it's simple really to send a text or a voice note, to stay in touch on a regular basis, and make time to see each other in person. It's being vulnerable with someone when you're struggling, and sharing the tears as well as the smiles. Relationships like that can light up a world and make it worth living.[12]

---

12. I am grateful to Mary Ann Kirkpatrick for her permission to include this extended response; email message to author, September 30, 2025.

Brief Reflections and Mini-Case Studies

* * *

What makes a meaningful relationship is deep friendship. It is a two-way interaction that fosters mutual understanding, a common sense of appreciation, and caring for the wellbeing of the other person. Deep friendship is a value that we have to foster in our interactions with other community members. One great example of this is going out of your way to ask how someone is doing, but then listening to what they have to say, acknowledging it, and sympathizing with anything they are sharing. If someone goes out of their way and is taking the time to know me at this level, I know they genuinely care about me as a person. It is also reciprocal; I will go out of my way to connect with friends, colleagues, etc., to understand how things are going for them, listen to what they have to share, acknowledge that, and converse with them to better understand what is going on with their lives. This fosters the value of deep friendship and is something that we care about and seek to foster with other community members. We take this even deeper by sharing and exploring with each other where we are at and what we are experiencing in our lives or personal paths together, which over time drives us to have deeper friendships or relationships with each other.[13]

* * *

Friendship is a gift, like prophecy or teaching. People with the gift of friendship have the ability to make the other person feel important and welcome. It is taking time and asking questions, and really listening to the answers. It is seeing and hearing what is said, and what is not said. It is a deep, unselfish interest in another person.
- I like friendships where I am neither intimidated nor do I intimidate; where I feel the power and the responsibility are equally shared.
- I like friendships that surprise me. I like to learn new things, to be challenged to bring novelty to the relationship.

13. Email message to author, September 30, 2025.

Appendix 13

- I like meeting with someone who has ideas to discuss and experiences to share.
- I do not like gossipy relationships or negative relationships. Some people spend their time complaining about other people in their lives (spouses, children, etc.). These people drag me into a critical attitude and I have to catch myself and turn the conversation. Sometimes this is done with a sense of humor, which makes it even harder.
- I like to laugh!
- I like this quote from Dinah Maria Mulock Craik:

"Oh, the comfort, the inexpressible comfort of feeling safe with a person; having neither to weigh thoughts nor measure words, but to pour them all out, just as they are, chaff and grain together, knowing that a faithful hand will take and sift them, keep what is worth keeping, and then, with a breath of kindness, blow the rest away."[14]

* * *

Commonalities start the relationship. Then comes effort to make the other feel special—laying down the red carpet (killing the fatted calf). Inclusion, being remembered, and being invited are essential as is honest conversation, talking about real life stuff, and not glossing over things.

It takes desire and effort to stay connected; even if time has passed, pick up in the connected place. And have a place in your heart that knows we are all human, not at all perfect but in our eyes the ones we love can do no wrong (unconditional love) even though you know they can.

Giving and receiving the benefit of the doubt helps. If something really goes sideways, have it in yourselves to resolve it no matter what. Respect that we all are different with different experiences and ideas formed by them. Placing the relationship above other things shows its importance. And then make time without having an

---

14. Email message to author, September 24, 2025. Dinah quote taken from Goodreads, "Dinah Maria Mulock Craik."

agenda—be truly there for the other person's needs and wants.[15]

Trust

The key to my good relationships revolves around the word "trust." Interestingly, the New Testament Greek words for faith and believing (*pistos* and *pisteo*) can also be translated by the words "trust" and "trusting." To believe in Jesus, for example, is to trust him. And trust is never blind, but is always based on personal experience where one knows that the other person is trustworthy.[16]

* * *

I believe that all positive relationships should be built on trust first in family, professional, and social relationships.

Family Relationships. As the first relationships that each of us develop as a human, these relationships are crucial as the building blocks for all future relationships we have. A child that experiences love, care, and physical and emotional nurture will most likely have the knowledge and experience for positive relationships throughout their lives. Romantic or spousal relationships are satisfying or fulfilling when you don't want or need those types of physical, emotional, or spiritual needs from some other source. That is what makes them meaningful, the acceptance or craving that your spouse or partner provides in that relationship.

Professional Relationships. Going on twenty-four years in the United States Army, I have learned that relationships built on trust and integrity are key to unit success. If your subordinates and supervisors can trust you to accomplish the mission, care for your soldiers and their families, and manage your equipment, that is what makes being a leader satisfying and fulfilling.

---

15. Email message to author, September 24, 2025.
16. Email message to author, September 24, 2025.

Appendix 13

Social or Civic Relationships. Law-abiding citizens are most likely to have positive relationships throughout the community if they have trust in one another. Having a community trust and respect each other makes for a positive environment for all those around them.[17]

Partnerships

We share similar beliefs and lifestyle. We have a deep love and respect for each other. We communicate well and care about each other's wellbeing. We are best friends. We share a long, rich history together. We value many of the same things, so that definitely helped shape the "bones" of our relationship. Added to that we have been able to invest a great deal of time together sharing recreation, service opportunities, and hosting study groups. Plus we've been able to transition the various seasons of life in a compatible way, so being together continues to be enjoyable after fifty-seven years. We feel listened to and appreciated, with both of those laying an important foundation for all the rest.[18]

* * *

Here's my thoughts on my relationship with my husband:
 It is meaningful because out of all the ladies out there he chose me. He starts the day with a kiss and ends the day with a kiss!
 It is satisfying because he is a good provider, father, grandfather, and husband. He is handy and resourceful.
 It is fulfilling because he takes those extra few seconds to compliment a good meal, thank me for helping him with a project, and thinks of my needs and wants as well as others.

---

17. Email message to author, September 24, 2025.
18. Email message to author, September 25, 2025.

Brief Reflections and Mini-Case Studies

If he won a million dollars he would help others in a heartbeat. He is a keeper![19]

* * *

For me, spending time together is important; we hold hands, walk together, share conversation, whatever we do is together. Knowing that I am his top choice and he is mine after fifty-five years is very satisfying. We met in college and love rehashing how we met. It was an instant attraction for both of us. Having and raising a family contributed to much contentment. It is very comforting to live with someone of my generation, with those values that are so different from today's folks. We both share and express our love through our gestures, speech, and deeds. We have a real commitment to each other and enjoy our life together. We take our marriage vows seriously.[20]

---

19. Email message to author, September 24, 2025.
20. Email message to author, September 25, 2025.

Appendix 14

Relationship Satisfaction Inventory (RSI)

INSTRUCTIONS: INDICATE THE EXTENT to which you are satisfied with your close personal relationships when considered together as a whole using a scale of 1–6 where "1" is "not at all, or never" satisfied and "6" is "completely, or always" satisfied. Please circle the number that best indicates your satisfaction with each aspect of your relationship.

In your close personal relationships as a whole, to what extent:	Not At All, Never					Completely, Always
1. Are you willing to invest and engage?	1	2	3	4	5	6
2. Is there emotional closeness and affection?	1	2	3	4	5	6
3. Do you experience trust and acceptance?	1	2	3	4	5	6
4. Do you experience care and support?	1	2	3	4	5	6

Relationship Satisfaction Inventory

5. Do you have similar and mutual interests?	1	2	3	4	5	6
6. Do you feel safe and comfortable?	1	2	3	4	5	6
7. Do you talk through and work out arguments and conflicts?	1	2	3	4	5	6
8. Are you open and do you feel understood in your communication?	1	2	3	4	5	6
9. Do you feel significant, important, or valued?	1	2	3	4	5	6
10. Does your relationship thrive or flourish?	1	2	3	4	5	6
11. Do you find enjoyment, pleasure, or contentment?	1	2	3	4	5	6

Scoring—First, add circled numbers for items 1–8 and divide by 8 to arrive at an average overall relationship satisfaction rating.

Next, add circled numbers for 2 items in each relational quality and divide total by 2 to arrive at an average relationship satisfaction rating for each quality as follows:

Communication—2 items (7, 8)
    Divide total score by 2 and enter average here: _____

Being Oneself—2 items (3, 5)
    Divide total score by 2 and enter average here: _____

Interpersonal Security and Warmth—2 items (2, 6)
    Divide total score by 2 and enter average here: _____

Support and Growth—2 items (1, 4)
    Divide total score by 2 and enter average here: _____

Appendix 14

Finally, circle the numbers for items 9–11 to determine how meaningful (item 9), satisfying (item 11), and fulfilling (item 10) are the close personal relationships.

Interpreting Results—Consider scores of 5 or 6 as "very satisfied" or "high" ratings, 3 or 4 as "moderately satisfied" or "average" ratings, and 1 or 2 as "not very satisfied" or "low" ratings.

Bibliography

Agnew, Christopher R., and Jennifer J. Harman, eds. *Power in Close Relationships*. New York: Cambridge University, 2019.

Berscheid, Ellen. "The Greening of Relationships Science." *American Psychologist* 54 (1999) 260–66.

Blasco-Belled, An. "Character Strengths and Mental Health as Complex Systems: A Network Analysis to Identify Bridge Strengths." *Current Psychology* 42 (2023) 25832–42.

Brooks, David. *How to Know a Person: The Art of Seeing Others Deeply and Being Deeply Seen*. New York: Random House, 2023.

Burns, David D. *Feeling Good Together: The Secret of Making Troubled Relationships Work*. New York: Broadway, 2008.

———. *Ten Days to Self-Esteem*. New York: HarperCollins, 1993.

Butler, Julie, and Margaret L. Kern. "The PERMA-Profiler: A Brief Multidimensional Measure of Flourishing." *International Journal of Wellbeing* 6 (2016) 1–48.

Caughlin, John P., and Ted L. Huston. "The Flourishing Literature on Flourishing Relationships." *The Journal of Family Theory and Review* 2 (2010) 25–35.

CFI Team. "What Is the PERMA Model?" Corporate Financial Institute. https://corporatefinanceinstitute.com/resources/management/perma-model.

Duck, Steven. *Handbook of Personal Relationships: Theory, Research and Interventions*. 2nd ed. New York: Wiley, 1997.

Everett, Percival. *James*. New York: Random House, 2024.

Fincham, Frank D., et al. "Relationship Satisfaction." In *The Cambridge Handbook of Personal Relationships*, edited by Anita L. Vangelisti and Daniel Perlman, 422–36. 2nd ed. Cambridge, UK: Cambridge University, 2018.

Fletcher, Garth J. O., and Julie Fitness, eds. *Knowledge Structures in Close Relationships: A Social Psychological Approach*. Mahwah, NJ: Lawrence Erlbaum Associates, 1996.

Bibliography

Funk, Janette L., and Ronald D. Rogge. "Testing the Ruler with Item Response Theory: Increasing Precision of Measurement for Relationship Satisfaction with the Couples Satisfaction Index." *Journal of Family Psychology* 21 (2007) 572–83.

Goodreads. "Dinah Maria Mulock Craik > Quotes > Quotable Quote." https://www.goodreads.com/quotes/219719-oh-the-comfort-the-inexpressible-comfort-of-feeling-safe-with.

Goza, Joel Edwards. *America's Unholy Ghosts: The Racist Roots of Our Faith and Politics.* Eugene, OR: Wipf & Stock, 2019.

Graham, James M., et al. "The Reliability of Relationship Satisfaction: A Reliability Generalization Meta-Analysis." *Journal of Family Psychology* 25 (2011) 39–48.

Harvey, Jennifer. *Dear White Christians: For Those Still Longing for Racial Reconciliation.* 2nd ed. Grand Rapids: Eerdmans, 2020.

Hawkley, Louise C., and John T. Cacioppo. "How Can I Connect with Thee: Measuring and Comparing Satisfaction in Multiple Relationship Domains." *Journal of Individual Psychology* 66 (2010) 43–58.

Hendrick, Susan S. "A Generic Measure of Relationship Satisfaction." *Journal of Marriage and the Family* 50 (1988) 91–98.

Kelley, Harold, et al., eds. *Close Relationships.* Clinton Corners, NY: Percheron, 2002.

Kimmerer, Robin Wall. *Braiding Sweetgrass: Indigenous Wisdom, Scientific Knowledge and the Teachings of Plants.* Minneapolis: Milkweed, 2013.

Kirkpatrick, Thomas G. *Better Ways to Better Relationships in the Church: Guidelines for Practicing Humility, Experiencing Empathy, Feeling Compassion, Showing Kindness, Expressing Appreciation, and Doing Justice.* Eugene, OR: Wipf & Stock, 2021.

———. *Communication in the Church: A Handbook for Creating Healthier Relationships.* Lanham, MD: Rowman and Littlefield, 2016.

———. "Conceptualizing and Developing Community in a Congregation." DMin diss., San Francisco Theological Seminary, 1978.

———. "Conceptualizing and Measuring Relationship Satisfaction." Paper presented at Western Speech Communication Association Convention, Phoenix, Arizona, February 20–23, 1977.

———. *Signs of Hope and Health in Mainline Churches: Guidelines for Creating Hopeful and Healthy Congregations.* Eugene, OR: Wipf & Stock, 2025.

Kwok, Pui-lan. *Postcolonial Imagination and Feminist Theology.* Louisville: Westminster John Knox, 2005.

Mashek, Debra J., and Arthur Aron, eds. *Handbook of Closeness and Intimacy.* Mahwah, NJ: Lawrence Erlbaum Associates, 2004.

Means, Casey, and Calley Means. *Good Energy: The Surprising Connection Between Metabolism and Limitless Health.* New York: Penguin Random House, 2024.

Merriam-Webster. "Fulfilling." https://www.merriam-webster.com/dictionary/fulfilling.

———. "Meaningful." https://www.merriam-webster.com/dictionary/meaningful.

Bibliography

———. "Satisfying." https://www.merriam-webster.com/dictionary/satisfying.

Naslund, Therese, and Sophia Reinholdsson. "The Features Behind Relationship Satisfaction in Friendship and Romantic Relationships." Master's thesis, Umea University, Sweden, 2016.

Nenquimo, Nemonte, and Mitch Anderson. *We Will Be Jaguars: A Memoir of My People*. New York: Abrams, 2024.

Niemiec, Ryan M. *Character Strengths Interventions: A Field Guide for Practitioners*. Boston: Hogrefe, 2017.

Niemiec, Ryan M., and Robert E. McGrath. *The Power of Character Strengths: Appreciate and Ignite Your Positive Personality*. Cincinnati: VIA Institute on Character, 2019.

Niemiec, Ryan M., and Ruth Pearce. "The Practice of Character Strengths: Unifying Definitions, Principles, and Exploration of What's Soaring, Emerging, and Ripe With Potential in Science and in Practice." *Frontiers in Psychology* 11 (2020). https://doi.org/10.3389/fpsyg.2020.590220.

Oxford English Dictionary. "Satisfying." https://www.oed.com/dictionary/satisfying_adj.

Oxford Learners Dictionaries. "Fulfilling." https://www.oxfordlearnersdictionaries.com/definition/english/fulfilling.

———. "Meaningful." https://www.oxfordlearnersdictionaries.com/definition/american_english/meaningful.

Paschalia, Mitskidou, et al. "Positive Relationships Questionnaire (PRQ): A Pilot Study." *Psychology* 12 (2021) 1039–57.

Peterson, Christopher, and Martin E. P. Seligman, eds. *Character Strengths and Virtues: A Handbook and Classification*. Oxford: American Psychological Association, 2004.

Positive Psychology Center. "PERMA Theory of Well-Being and PERMA Workshops." https://ppc.sas.upenn.edu/learn-more/perma-theory-well-being-and-perma-workshops.

Pransky, George S. *The Relationship Handbook: A Simple Guide to Satisfying Relationships*. La Conner, WA: Pransky and Associates, 2001.

Reis, Harry T., et al. "Ellen Berscheid, Elaine Hatfield, and the Emergence of Relationship Science." *Perspectives on Psychological Science* 8 (2013) 558–72.

Richo, David. *How to Be an Adult in Relationships: The Five Keys to Mindful Loving*. Boulder, CO: Shambhala, 2021.

Ruiz, Don Miguel, et al. *The Fifth Agreement: A Practical Guide to Self-Mastery*. San Rafael, CA: Amber-Allen, 2011.

Russo-Netzer, Pninit. "Why You Should Prioritize Meaning in Your Life." Greater Good, March 6, 2019. https://greatergood.berkeley.edu/article/item/why_you_should_prioritize_meaning_in_your_everyday_life.

Seligman, Martin E. P. *Authentic Happiness: Using the New Positive Psychology to Realize Your Potential for Lasting Fulfillment*. New York: Free Press, 2002.

———. *Flourish: A Visionary New Understanding of Happiness and Well-Being*. New York: Free Press, 2011.

Bibliography

Simpson, Jeffry A., and Lorne Campbell, eds. *The Oxford Handbook of Close Relationships*. New York: Oxford, 2013.

Steger, Michael F., and Pninit Russo-Netzer. "To Have Your Best Life, Do You Need to Be Your Best Self?" VIA Institute on Character. https://www.viacharacter.org/topics/articles/to-have-your-best-life-do-you-need-to-be-your-best-you.

Sternberg, Robert J., and Mahzad Hojjat, eds. *Satisfaction in Close Relationships*. New York: Guilford, 1997.

Suttie, Jill. "Four Keys to a Meaningful Life." Greater Good, January 20, 2017. https://greatergood.berkeley.edu/article/item/four_keys_to_a_meaningful_life.

———. "Seven Ways to Find Your Purpose in Life." Greater Good, August 6, 2020. https://greatergood.berkeley.edu/article/item/seven_ways_to_find_your_purpose_in_life.

Suttie, Jill, and Jason Marsh. "Is a Happy Life Different from a Meaningful One?" Greater Good, February 25, 2014. https://greatergood.berkeley.edu/article/item/happy_life_different_from_meaningful_life.

Van Tongeren, Daryl R., and Jeni L. Burnette. "Do You Believe Happiness Can Change? An Investigation of the Relationship Between Happiness Mindsets, Well-Being, and Satisfaction." *The Journal of Positive Psychology* 13 (2018) 101–9.

Van Tongeren, Daryl R., et al. "Prosociality Enhances Meaning in Life." *The Journal of Positive Psychology* 11 (2016) 225–36.

Van Tongeren, Daryl R., and Sara A. Showalter Van Tongeren. *The Courage to Suffer: A New Clinical Framework for Life's Greatest Crises*. West Conshohocken, PA: Templeton, 2020.

VanderDrift, Laura E., et al. "Friendship and Romance: A Need-Fulfillment Perspective." In *The Psychology of Friendship*, edited by Mahzad Hojjat and Anne Moyer, 109–22. New York: Oxford University, 2017.

Vangelisti, Anita L., and Daniel Perlman. *The Cambridge Handbook of Personal Relationships*. 2nd ed. Cambridge, UK: Cambridge University, 2018.

VIA Institute on Character. "Honesty." https://www.viacharacter.org/character-strengths/honesty.

———. "How Do Character Strengths Improve Happiness." Email from via@viacharacter.org, November 14, 2023.

Wilkerson, Isabel. *Caste: The Origins of Our Discontents*. New York: Random House, 2020.

Wink, Walter. *The Powers That Be: Theology for a New Millennium*. New York: Doubleday, 1999.

Wood, Julia T. *Interpersonal Communication in Everyday Encounters*. 9th ed. Boston: Cengage Learning, 2019.

———. *Relational Communication*. Belmont, CA: Wadsworth, 1995.

Wright, Paul H. "A Bare-Bones Guide to the Acquaintance Description Form-F2." Paul H. Wright, November 1997. paulhwright.com.

Bibliography

———. "The Acquaintance Description Form." In *Understanding Personal Relationships: An Interdisciplinary Approach*, edited by Steven Duck and Daniel Perlman, 39–62. London: Sage, 1985.

Zimbardo, Philip. "Seven Paths to a Meaningful Life." Greater Good, May 28, 2013. https://greatergood.berkeley.edu/article/item/seven_paths_to_a_meaningful_life.

www.ingramcontent.com/pod-product-compliance
Lightning Source LLC
Chambersburg PA
CBHW060820190426
43197CB00038B/2162